Be More POLLYANNA

Essays & Ideas to Inspire Intentional Gladness

HOLLY TERRILL

Be More Pollyanna: Essays & Ideas to Inspire Intentional Gladness

Copyright © 2025 Holly Terrill

Published by Quiet Storm Services, LLC
P.O. Box 20505
Wichita, KS 67208
www.quietstormservices.com

ISBN: 979-8-9860051-2-6
Library of Congress Control Number: 2025907413
First Edition. August 2025.
Cover Design: Gina Laiso
Cover Artist: Cynthia Martinez-Woelk
Foreword: Cody Custer
Editor: Katie Dakan

All rights reserved. No part of this publication may be reproduced, distributed, or transmitted in any form or by any means, including photocopying, recording, or other electronic/mechanical methods, without the prior written permission of the copyright holder.

This book is creative nonfiction. It reflects the author's present recollections of experiences over time. Some names and characteristics may have been changed, some events may have been compressed, and some dialogue may have been recreated.
Chat GPT was utilized to adapt the content for the back cover.

SBW

"I may not have gone where I intended to go, but I think I have ended up where I needed to be."

– Douglas Adams

Contents

Foreword..9

Introduction..13

Who is Pollyanna?..................................15

1. The Bright Side (Without the Rose-Colored Glasses) – Optimism........................19

2. Steady in the Storm – Equilibrium..............37

3. Reading the Room (and Yourself, Too) – Emotional Intelligence..................59

4. Filling Your Own Cup – Self-Care................79

5. Kindness as a Superpower – Compassion...101

6. Letting Go & Leaning In – Acceptance.......121

7. The People Who Shape Us – Relationships...143

8. Living Unapologetically – Authenticity.....163

9. Bouncing Back – Resilience........................185

10. A Pollyanna State of Mind - Zen...............209

Afterword...233

About the Author................................236

Acknowledgements.............................237

References..240

Resources...242

Foreword

Be more like Pollyanna, whimsical and wise: finding the good in the shit. Why is a child's impulsive and almost limit-free energy so often thrown to the side as if optional to life? Frequently, adults feel the weight and bounds of "adulting" while simultaneously not putting intention or time into this child's approach of breathing life into the everyday. They are interconnected, and Holly Terrill takes a human and practical approach to this intentional choice of being glad and finding fulfillment in the everyday.

In the following pages, you will journey from peaks of laughter to the darker side of joy, trying to find the nuggets in their story and how they live a simple idea, to find joy and happiness in the silver lining, no matter what. Inspiration for this work is pulled from the novel *Pollyanna* and the character Pollyanna's "Glad Game" based on the idea I loosely translate to: "Find the good in the shit no matter what, there is always some."

I knew Holly first as a friend of a friend, and even then, I could see this youthful exuberance from the outside, from the unknown. I grew to know them on Sundays through a group of friends who would meet to counsel each other on our weekly woes. Each time, Holly would bring a nugget of joy, life, love, and often the best dark humor, exhibiting this external practice of the "Glad Game." I now see Holly almost every day as their coworker and friend; trust me - they live this in every moment.

This finding of joy and happiness is in their blood and every breath they breathe. No matter what meeting we are in, whether brainstorming, working with people of all walks of life, or debriefing from a tense encounter, Holly simply and amazingly shows it can be done anywhere. In these moments, books like Be More Pollyanna effectively and sincerely simplify a topic often overlooked: positivity.

Ideally, the words and wisdom become accessible to all who are willing to laugh a little more, dance even one step, or wear the outfit you want but second-guess because of others' possible opinions. The fleeting time we have to live a life of joy is easy to miss and critical to celebrate. Holly combines personal anecdotes filled with hardships and challenges with stories of family, failures, and festivities, and brings you to the table with challenges for your daily journey. Some of these challenges will take time while reuniting you with pen, paper, and progress in the written form. Some of these challenges will bring you to stop the storm in your brain long enough to see the flower pot in a neighborhood you walk through every day and miss.

The idea is simple in both writing and practice: find joy, and you will bring to light the gems that already exist in your day-to-day life. Perhaps you will find a path filled with laughter and light.

Cody Custer,
December 2024

Introduction

This book is about more than just staying positive. It's about learning to recognize the good—even in difficult, messy, or painful circumstances—without ignoring reality or pretending everything is fine. Life can be hard. Terrible things happen. But even then, it's possible to find clarity, meaning, and purpose.

Throughout these pages, I share essays, poems, and personal stories that reflect this mindset. For much of my life, my natural optimism was dismissed or misunderstood. But those experiences, instead of dimming my outlook, deepened it. They became the foundation for this book.

When I lost my job in early 2023 after two decades in the financial services sector, I faced a moment that could have left me stuck in fear and doubt. Instead, I leaned into my emotions, made a plan, and chose growth. I read, studied, and volunteered over 200 hours in just a few months. It wasn't easy—especially when battling insomnia and medication shortages—but I found my way back to myself.

Writing has always been part of who I am. From childhood stories to NaNoWriMo novels typed at Starbucks while my baby napped, the desire to share words never left me. But this book felt different. When the idea for intentional gladness came, I knew I had to see it through—not just for myself, but for people like you who are seeking light, hope, and momentum.

In these pages, you'll find not only stories and poetry but also ideas and exercises for reflection. Look for the phrase "Te toca a ti! – It's your turn!" when it's time to pause and apply what you've read. I hope this book gives you tools to uncover joy, even in unexpected places. Please feel empowered to jot down your thoughts in the margins of this book, or if you prefer, have a notebook or paper, and writing utensils at hand.

I'm glad you're here.

Who is Pollyanna?

When I began drafting this book, I realized that I had never actually read *Pollyanna* or seen Disney's 1960 movie adaptation starring Hayley Mills. People have regularly told me they attribute my cheerful disposition to being Pollyanna-ish. From what I had heard of the story, I came to understand that using this word was intended to negatively interpret my positive outlook as naïve or ignorant of reality. This glib assessment, from casual observers and the people whose feedback mattered, could not be further from the truth.

American author Eleanor H. Porter wrote *Pollyanna*, which was first published in 1913. It is the story of a girl named Pollyanna Whittier, who comes to live with her spinster aunt after becoming orphaned. Upon initial observation, Pollyanna appears to be an eternal optimist. Only through learning more about her relationship with her deceased father can we better understand that Pollyanna's optimism is not a youthful or ignorant attribute of her character, but a constant, intentional focus taught to her through a game introduced by her father.

In Porter's book, Pollyanna's father teaches her appreciation by focusing on positivity using a tool he calls "The Glad Game." Pollyanna and her father were extremely poor. They often got supplies from barrels full of donated goods. During one of these trips to look through a barrel of goods, Pollyanna, hoping to find a doll, instead found a pair of crutches. She is disappointed because she does not need crutches. Pollyanna's father reframes the situation by telling Pollyanna that she should be glad she does not need crutches because that means she is healthy.

From this moment on, Pollyanna and her father play The Glad Game in every situation they can to help direct their focus on what is optimistic about a situation. When her father passes away and she is sent to live with her mother's sister, Aunt Polly, Pollyanna expresses that she is glad to have the opportunity to live with a relative who will love and care for her. Pollyanna's constant attention to her attitude and how she perceives negativity helps those around her to begin to do the same. In a town where several community members continually gripe about their various struggles, Pollyanna refuses to be drawn into their pattern of whining or complaining. Instead, she redirects their attention to the lessons that can be learned through hardship.

The Glad Game gives Pollyanna a unique opportunity to see things from a point of view that may not come naturally to her. Each time she plays the game with someone new, she helps that individual better understand their experiences and, in turn, creates another gladness rebel. I use the word rebel here because rebels are non-conformists, much like punk rockers. Individuals seeking out gladness when it's easier to succumb to sadness fight the status quo; they are positivity warriors.

I have regularly practiced the Glad Game without identifying it as such. My practice often includes the statement "at least." I used to have a daily calendar called *Advice from a Unicorn*. I do not believe it is manufactured anymore, but at least I enjoyed the daily affirmations for a little while. See what I did there? I have heard that using the statement "at least" can diminish a person's experience, and that could be the case. Although I have interpreted it to mean that I recognize a situation and deliberately identify a way in which I was fortunate in it.

I saved the daily calendar pages and used them as notes to my coworkers, friends, and even my kiddo. A while back, my son pulled out one of the notes from his backpack and turned to the friend sitting with him in the backseat of our car.

"My mom always writes me notes on these when there is something important to share," he explained. He is not wrong; I search for the most appropriate daily affirmation for the situation at hand and write a personalized note on the back.

My favorite daily affirmation from the three years I used the calendar was: "Growing up is a sham, but do it well anyway." When I first read it, and even now when I re-read it, I think to myself, *"Adulting may be hard, but at least I made it to adulthood; There are many people who never got the chance to grow up and live their lives, and I get to. For that, I am glad.*

Chapter 1

The Bright Side
(Without the Rose-Colored Glasses)

*Explore the power of optimism
in fostering intentional gladness.*

Picture for a moment, two individuals facing identical challenges, yet their experiences could not be more different. One person may be consumed by despair, while the other person radiates a resilient joy that seems unbreakable. What do you think sets them apart?

The secret lies in the transformative power of optimism, a power we are about to tackle together in the pages that follow. Reverie is the tool we will use, and changed behavior, while not always easy, is the action that can help us harness this power and steer us toward a life of intentional gladness.

What I Like About Me

In the hustle and bustle of daily life, it is easy to overlook our own strengths and positive qualities. Yet acknowledging these attributes is crucial for personal growth and self-empowerment. I quickly identify three core strengths: my natural positivity, my authenticity, and my love for smiling. By recognizing and embracing these qualities, and by adding more to my list, I hope to foster a deeper sense of self-worth and resilience.

One of my most significant strengths is my natural positivity. I have always been inclined to see the silver lining in every situation, no matter how challenging. This positive outlook helps me navigate through tough times and uplifts those around me. In my volunteer experience and in the workplace, this quality has proven invaluable. It fosters a collaborative environment, motivates my team, and enables us to tackle problems with a solution-oriented mindset.

Every morning, I intentionally acknowledge that I am a naturally positive person. Like Pollyanna, I strive to maintain a positive outlook, which not only enhances my own well-being but also spreads positivity to those around me. This simple practice sets the tone for my day, allowing me to approach each task with energy and optimism. It is this unwavering positivity that has often turned potential setbacks into opportunities for growth and learning.

Another cornerstone of my character is authenticity. I believe in being true to myself and others, which means expressing my thoughts and feelings honestly. This trait has earned me the trust and respect of my peers and loved ones. Authenticity, however, is not just about honesty; it is also about embracing my true self, including my strengths and imperfections. Pollyanna's authenticity shines through in her interactions with others. She is genuine and sincere, which endears her to the people she meets. By acknowledging that I am authentic, I reinforce my commitment to living a genuine life. This reminder empowers me to maintain integrity and uphold personal values, even when faced with societal pressures to conform. For example, when witnessing injustice, I commit to speaking up, regardless of how the individuals around me react. In professional settings, my authenticity fosters transparent communication and builds strong, trust-based relationships.

My immense love for smiling is more than just a habit; it reflects my positive energy and warm personality. Smiling is a simple yet profound expression of joy and kindness. A smile can create a welcoming atmosphere, even in the most difficult of settings. It is a universal language that conveys goodwill and fosters connections.

Pollyanna's infectious smile and joyful demeanor have a transformative effect on the people around her, teaching them to find happiness in the small things. Each day, as I acknowledge that I love to smile, I remind myself of the great power of this small act. It encourages me to spread positivity and kindness, making the world around me a little brighter. Whether I am spending time with my family, greeting a colleague, or interacting with a stranger, my smile is a testament to my optimistic spirit and genuine care for others. As I continue this practice of self-compassion, I strive to expand my personal inventory of strengths and positive qualities.

Here are five more that I choose to acknowledge and celebrate:

- Empathy: I have a deep understanding of others' emotions and perspectives, which allows me to offer support and compassion.

- Resilience: I possess the ability to bounce back from adversity, learn from each experience and grow stronger.

- Creativity: I bring innovative ideas and solutions to the table, enhancing both my personal and professional endeavors.

- Dedication: I am committed to my goals and responsibilities, putting in the effort and perseverance needed to achieve success.

- Kindness: I prioritize acts of kindness and strive to make a positive impact on those around me.

By regularly reflecting on these qualities, I reinforce my belief in them and integrate them more deeply into my self-concept. This practice not only boosts my confidence but also motivates me to continue growing and evolving. Acknowledging and affirming our strengths is a powerful tool for personal development. Drawing inspiration from Pollyanna, I embrace the positive qualities that make life joyful and meaningful. As I expand my inventory of strengths, I embrace a fuller, more empowered version of myself. This daily practice fosters resilience, optimism, and a deeper connection to my true self, guiding me toward a more fulfilling and glad life.

Love is an Action

Something I do regularly is sing and dance, which embarrasses my teenager when we are out in public. I like to treat my life as if it is a musical, so I make up songs about what I am doing or what is happening around me. I can't contain myself when I hear a song that I enjoy—and I enjoy a lot of songs. We have a tradition of taking our kiddo out to dinner after school functions; I call it "forced family fun." On one such occasion, I sat down in the booth at the restaurant beside my son. He made a disappointed sound that was a literal "ugh." It made me smile; teenagers are so easy to annoy.

My spouse sat down across from us; obviously, there was no way the booth was going to fit three adult-sized bodies. A brief time after we got our dinners, a song came on the radio at the restaurant that I liked. I started to sing along between bites of gluten-free macaroni 'n' cheese. "Stooopppp," came the response from my right to my belting out the lyrics to whatever song it was. I replied with the only thing that felt appropriate. "I can't," I said. Then, to add more oomph to my performance, I moved my head and shoulders in a dance choreography of my own design. I do not think I have ever been self-conscious of people seeing my dance moves, as terrible as they might be. My kid let out another "ugh" and then picked up his dinner and moved to an adjacent table.

He ate alone for about five minutes but eventually returned to the table, resigned to the fact that his mom would continue to be authentically themself. We were the only people in the restaurant that night, but honestly, I would have behaved the same way even if patrons occupied every table.

My grandmother used to sing all the time. And when she was not singing, she was humming. I do not know if she could whistle (I cannot), but I only remember her singing or humming. One time, when I was young, my grandma was in the kitchen making her annual Thanksgiving chili, and I was playing on the stairs at the back of the room. I cannot recall if I mentioned her singing or if she just wanted to share, but she said to me, "*I may not have a great singing voice, but I have a lot of heart.*" I am my grandmother's grandkid. I may be tone-deaf, but that does not stop me from singing with a joyful heart.

In 2021, the pop-punk band Green Day released a song called *Pollyanna*. I love the lyrics; they are vulnerable and pure. The imagery my mind creates while listening to the lyrics is a visual compilation of raw but hopeful images, calling out the struggles many of us had while craving positive social interaction and wading through mental and physical health crises during a time when most of the world was still in some form of social isolation due to the COVID-19 pandemic. I love this song so much. I fondly recollect taking solitary walks during my lunch break—headphones in, volume up, bopping along to the beat as I strolled along the tree-lined walking path near my house. This song gave me optimism for a brighter, post-pandemic future.

Finding Clarity, Inspiration, and Purpose in Daily Rituals

My favorite time of day for daydreaming or visualizing positive outcomes is during the tranquil solitude of my morning shower. It is a daily ritual—my daily sanctuary, which lasts for a brief time but greatly benefits me. Exceptions are rare; only on Easter and Christmas mornings have I had to leap out of bed and into action before the water had a chance to cascade over me. The

Easter Bunny and Old St. Nick have now retreated from our lives, leaving me grateful for the return of 365 mornings of uninterrupted deliberation.

Once I step into the shower, the warmth of the water envelops me, and I let my mind wander. *Have I retained any fragments of last night's dreams? If so, what surreal tales have my subconscious spun?* In my forties, my dreams have produced a realm of oddities and impossibilities, and I often find myself marveling at their eccentricity. These dreams, filled with vibrant colors and peculiar scenarios, sometimes leave me pondering their deeper meanings. *Is my subconscious trying to tell me something? Are these dreams a reflection of my desires, fears, or merely random neural firings?*

After musing over my dreams, I shift my focus to the day ahead. *What is on the schedule that requires my attention? Are there any presentations or speeches to deliver? Do I need to gather supplies for activities before or after work/volunteering/school? Do I have parental responsibilities to keep in mind?* There is always something to plan and prepare for. I mentally walk through my tasks, organizing them in a way that feels manageable. This preparation helps me feel more in control, turning potential chaos into a structured plan. I know I cannot prepare for every possibility, but I like to be prepared when it is doable.

The flowing water lulls me into a meditative state where I envision myself with the means to achieve, accomplish, and succeed. Instances of introspection like this exist solely within these short minutes. I imagine myself confidently delivering a presentation, my words flowing smoothly and engaging my audience. I see myself navigating challenges with grace and finding creative solutions to problems that may arise. These visualizations are more than just idle fantasies; they are blueprints for success, shaping my mindset and boosting my confidence.

When I turn the lever and the water ceases to flow, I am pulled back to reality, but I carry with me the determination kindled by the sensations that momentarily enveloped me. The clarity I gain from this ritual provides a sense of direction, and the inspiration fuels my motivation throughout the day. In those fleeting moments beneath the warmth of the flowing water, I find clarity, inspiration, and the strength to face the day.

This practice keeps me grounded and fosters a sense of purpose, reminding me of the boundless potential we all possess when we take time to reflect and dream, even if it is just for a few minutes each morning. The shower, a simple everyday activity transforms into a sacred space where I nurture my dreams and ambitions. This ritual, though brief, has a profound impact on my outlook and helps me navigate the complexities of life with a clear mind and an inspired heart.

The Power of Positive Intentions

Setting positive intentions is a deeply personal practice that has the power to shape our outlook and influence our actions. These intentions can serve as our guiding stars, helping us maintain focus, motivation, and a positive mindset throughout the days and weeks ahead. Aligning our intentions with our values and priorities can create a roadmap to a more fulfilling and productive life. The practice of setting intentions goes beyond merely hoping for the best; it involves a conscious commitment to certain attitudes and behaviors that can transform our experiences and interactions.

Positive intentions come in many forms. Some I have prioritized in my life include gratitude, positivity, productivity, self-care, kindness, mindfulness, learning, creativity, health, connection, adaptability, organization, generosity, resilience, and joy. Though not exhaustive, this list provides a starting point for crafting intentions that resonate with us. Each intention carries its unique energy and potential to enrich our lives. For instance, an intention centered on gratitude can shift our focus from what we lack to what we have, fostering a sense of abundance and contentment. On the other hand, an intention to be more organized can streamline our daily routines, reducing stress and increasing efficiency.

In my daily practice of setting positive intentions, I often gravitate toward more than one theme. Positivity and learning flow naturally for me, and depending on the season of life, gratitude and joy come effortlessly as well. However, I recognize that categories like self-care, physical health, and organization require more conscious effort and intention for me. Self-care might involve deliberately setting aside time to rest and recharge despite a busy schedule. Physical health might mean consistently exercising and eating nutritiously, even when it is inconvenient. Organization skills might require the discipline to declutter and create systems that support productivity, which is not an easy ask of myself.

Years ago, I delved into *The Happiness Project* by Gretchen Rubin—a captivating chronicle of her yearlong quest to enhance her overall happiness and life satisfaction. The book inspired me and served as a reminder that time moves swiftly, even on days that seem endless. Rubin's meticulous approach to improving different areas of her life, month by month, resonated deeply with me. Her journey underscored the importance of intentionality in the pursuit of happiness and provided me with practical insights that I could apply in my own life. As a naturally optimistic person, I felt compelled to share my positivity systematically and purposefully with others. This realization led me to become more intentional in my practices around positivity.

Expressing gratitude for my job and its opportunities empowered me to uplift my teammates. I began to see my workplace not only as a place of employment, but a community where positive energy could thrive. Approaching challenges with a positive mindset and actively seeking solutions rather than dwelling on roadblocks has provided a significant advantage in my strategic planning endeavors. I have enabled myself to tackle obstacles with creativity and resilience in more places than simply at work.

Making healthier choices and incorporating brief exercise breaks into each day infused me with more energy to spend quality time with my family. These small, intentional actions collectively enhanced my overall well-being. They contributed to a more harmonious balance between work, volunteering, and personal life. A daily practice centered on positive intentions can enrich an individual's life and create a ripple effect in the lives of those they touch. We can foster a more progressive and interconnected world by judging ourselves through our intentions and choosing to assume positive intent in others.

It is not solely about thinking positively, but about living with intention and sharing the resulting optimism with those around us. When we are mindful of how our attitudes and actions impact our surroundings, we can cultivate an environment of support and encouragement. By embracing positive intentions, we can contribute to a collective atmosphere of growth and positivity, where everyone can feel inspired to bring out the best in themselves and others.

happiness is a bonfire

autumn had yet to truly arrive

its colorful transformation sprinkled sparsely

throughout the city

patches of red and orange peering out at me

through sleep-deprived eyes

exhaustion set in

a dire need

for a few moments of calm a fire - the remedy

the reminder

that the day called for an early afternoon bonfire

Te toca a ti! – It's your turn!

Over a week, embark on an optimism experiment to explore its influence on fostering intentional gladness. Each morning, as you start your day, begin by setting a positive intention for the waking hours ahead. As you encounter challenges, setbacks, or moments of stress, consciously choose to reframe your perspective optimistically. For example, if you are faced with a challenging task, remember that challenges offer opportunities for growth and learning.

This experiment encourages you to actively engage with the concept of optimism and its role in shaping your emotional responses and overall gladness. By consciously practicing optimism, you gain valuable insights into its potential to transform your perspective and enhance your experience of joy.

Chapter 2

Steady in the Storm

Explore the importance of stability in various areas of life for sustained gladness.

Imagine a tightrope walker, perched high above the ground, inching their way across a thin, swaying rope. In one hand, they hold the weight of responsibilities—career, family, and ambition—while the other hand clings to dreams of leisure time, self-care, and personal passions. Their journey is a precarious dance between these two realms, and every step forward demonstrates their ability to maintain equilibrium.

Like that tightrope walker, each of us travels a unique path, trying to balance the demands of our daily lives with the desire for inner peace and contentment. It is a universal struggle, and the stakes are high. One misstep can lead to exhaustion, burnout, or a nagging sense of unfulfillment.

In the following pages, we will explore the multifaceted nature of balance—how it encompasses not only the allocation of time, but also the alignment of values, the cultivation of mindfulness, and the nurturing of our physical and emotional well-being.

Secure Your Oxygen Mask First

Before the pandemic, I was on a plane with coworkers headed for a work conference in Washington, D.C. I was in my seat, talking excitedly to a teammate about all the sightseeing I wanted to cram into our short trip, while simultaneously posting photos of the view from my plane to social media. The flight attendant went into their usual instructional safety announcement, explaining where the emergency exits were located and what to do in case of a water landing. When they got to the section of the safety speech that talked about oxygen masks, I stopped scrolling on Facebook and looked up at the flight attendant who was presenting.

I had heard this spiel before, but this time it was as if I was hearing it for the first time. It went something like this:

"Air pressure in the cabin is being monitored. In the event of decompression, an oxygen mask will automatically appear in front of you. To start the flow of oxygen, pull the mask toward you. Place it firmly over your nose and mouth, secure the elastic band behind your head, and breathe normally. Although the bag may not inflate, oxygen is flowing to the mask. If you are

traveling with a child or someone who requires assistance, secure your mask first, and then assist the other person."

Until then, I would have said it was selfish to take care of me first. I am a leader; I am responsible for prioritizing others on my team. But now a stranger was expecting me to take care of my safety before attempting to care for others. When I stopped and thought about it for a moment, I wondered why I was not already doing this in every aspect of my life. This was great advice; I felt I had been given permission to take care of myself!

Workplaces can be places of high stress on the best of days. When (*when,* not *if*) things go wrong—such as employee callouts, technology troubles, or even attempts to continue business during a pandemic—unprecedented levels of pressure are placed on employees, volunteers, and their leaders. As leaders, it is our responsibility to keep our teammates motivated, refreshed, challenged, and engaged. However, we will not be up for the gig if we, too, are exhausted, lack motivation, or have become disconnected from our work.

An example of good leadership is modeling the behaviors we wish to see in our teammates.

By taking care of ourselves, we reinforce the importance of wellness to our teams. Below are five areas I choose to focus on to help improve my mental, emotional, and physical health. These tips have been helpful for me, and may help you too!

- Get enough sleep. I have heard the phrase "I'll sleep when I'm dead" plenty of times over the years; there just always seems to be too much to do and never enough time. We must understand how critical a good night's sleep is to help for proper rest and rejuvenation. As the Dalai Lama said, *"Sleep is the best meditation."*

- Make sure to move around every now and again. During the day, stick your earbuds in and rock out to a few tunes to help you feel motivated. Or choose to take advantage of the few short moments in the elevator at work to dance like nobody's watching. I like to listen to music and dance around my house while I am getting ready for work in the morning. Going for a walk before work, during a lunch break, or after work can also do the trick.

- Laugh (a lot). When I was in high school, I saw an advertisement in an Entertainment Weekly magazine. The advertisement said: *"Laughter is the best medicine. Unless you're really sick, then you should call 9-1-1."* I ripped the page out of the magazine and taped it to my wall. Since then, it's moved with me from home to home, and it now resides in my home office as part of an art collage I made while completing my undergraduate studies. The advertisement reminds me of the importance of laughter and finding joy in all things. Laughter soothes tension, improves moods, and even releases endorphins. It also feels good to make others laugh. I highly recommend it.

- Pay attention to what you put in your head. Positive self-talk can enhance confidence, boost performance, and improve one's mood. Leadership is about helping others recognize the greatness within themselves. If I am more confident, I can share that confidence with those I lead. When negative thoughts fill my mind, I find it most helpful to reframe these thoughts into positive ones. If I am feeling unproductive,

I remove those feelings of inadequacy by reminding myself of all I have accomplished during the day and finding something to be grateful for in my life.

- Find a hobby—unleash your creativity. Hobbies are activities we do because we want to, not because we must. Creativity enables us to look at things differently, and to solve problems in new and innovative ways. Whether it is reading, writing, painting, or any other hobby, these activities give us an outlet to enjoy our passions and release tension. One of my favorite past hobbies was playing the ukulele; I am a novice for sure, but I love it.

Changing habits can feel uncomfortable; it is easier to ignore what is different than it is to change our habits. Give these steps a chance, and I bet you will feel healthier and less stressed just by taking a little better care of you. Just as the flight attendant instructed me to put my mask on first, I am empowering you. The best we can do as leaders, and people, is to take care of ourselves—physically, emotionally, and mentally—to support the people in our lives counting on us.

Breaking the Chains: My Rivalry with Writer's Block

Writer's block—a dreaded mental obstacle that stands between a writer and their creative potential—has plagued wordsmiths throughout history. It is that frustrating moment when your mind feels like a barren desert, devoid of ideas and inspiration. However, it is crucial to remember that writer's block is not an insurmountable force. With the right strategies and mindset, breaking free from its grasp can reignite creativity. Overcoming writer's block helps unleash our inner storyteller.

The blank page can be daunting for me, but it is also an opportunity waiting to be seized. Instead of viewing it as an empty void, I strive to see it as a canvas where I can paint my thoughts and ideas. To combat the fear of imperfection, a main contributor to writer's block, I allow myself to write badly at first. I start by jotting down anything that comes to mind, even if it seems trivial or disjointed. Over time, these fragments can evolve into a coherent narrative—even an essay or story that ends up printed in a book about intentional gladness—see what I did there?

Setting unrealistic expectations can lead to paralysis. I tend to break my writing goals into smaller, achievable tasks and focus on completing a single paragraph or section at a time, with word number goals or a time deadline. I celebrate small victories to build momentum, which has the power to propel me past the writer's block mentality. Sometimes a change of scenery can work wonders. If I am stuck in a writer's block rut, I relocate to a different room, a café, or even a park.

Fresh surroundings can stimulate creativity and offer new perspectives. By removing myself from distractions I can concentrate on my writing. Honestly though, if I pull my cell phone out at any time during my scheduled writing time, distractions abound. So, if you are like me, keep that tiny computer hidden from reach. Freewriting is a technique where a person writes without any specific purpose or structure for a set period, often between five to fifteen minutes. During this time, I let my thoughts flow freely onto the page without judgment. My goal is not to create a masterpiece, but to bypass my inner critic and encourage ideas to emerge.

I am often surprised by the gems buried within my unfiltered stream of consciousness. I typically try this technique early in the day when I still have fragments of the previous night's dreams lingering within reach of consciousness. My inspiration comes from various sources. I read books, watch television (Netflix and Disney are my go-to streaming channels), I listen to music, and explore what resonates with me. These experiences can spark innovative ideas and breathe life into my writing.

I also enjoy engaging in discussions with my friends, colleagues, and fellow writers to help me see my work from different angles and overcome creative blocks. I have found that my friends are the most difficult bunch to talk about my writing with. It may be because they do not want to be critical of me, attempting to save me from unwanted negative feelings. Consistency is key to overcoming writer's block. I attempt to establish a writing routine that fits my lifestyle and stick to it. Regular, consistent practice conditions my mind to be more receptive to creative ideas when I sit down to write. For instance, I committed to writing a blog for 100 days in the months before my forty-first birthday; I got to day 75 before needing to take a respite due to the demands of my work schedule at the time.

Writing is a process, and the first draft is going to be less than perfect. I must give myself permission to write with the understanding that revisions will refine my work. When I initially began editing the first draft of this book, I began with the intention to cut approximately 10 percent of the story. In my haste, I cut everything—forcing me to start again from scratch. The book you hold in your hands is vastly different from the original. The freedom to edit and improve later can alleviate the pressure of producing flawless prose from the start. Who knows, one day I might go back and rewrite that original manuscript as a compilation of essays.

What I am hoping I expressed is that writer's block is a formidable adversary, but it is not invincible. By embracing the blank page, setting realistic goals, changing my writing environment, practicing free form writing, seeking inspiration outside myself, establishing a routine, and, finally, accepting my revisions, I can break free from its grip and unleash my creative potential. While I am sure that every writer faces this challenge, it is the determination to overcome it that separates the aspiring from the accomplished. So, join me in the accomplished writers' circle and go forth with confidence—for the words you seek are within you, waiting to be written.

Harmonizing Passion and Profit

In today's world, personal values play a pivotal role in shaping our lives and careers. For me, values that encompass Diversity, Equity, Inclusion, and Belonging (DEIB) hold significant importance. While pursuing a career in banking may not seem like an obvious path for aligning with these values, there were numerous ways for a person such as myself to incorporate them into both my professional and personal life. In my former banking career, I helped promote DEIB by advocating for change within my workplace. I encouraged my employers to diversify their talent pools by seeking out candidates from varied backgrounds and abilities. This enriches the workforce and sends a strong message about our commitment to DEIB.

Years ago, I established a mentorship program within my department to support employees in advancing their career through knowledge and professionalism. This initiative provided guidance, support, and opportunities for professional growth, helping to bridge the diversity and equity gap that existed throughout the organization. By directing capital toward projects that benefit marginalized communities, the financial banking industry can become a force for positive change. I have strived to encourage my employers to consider the social and environmental impacts of their investments, and to align them with principles of equity and sustainability.

Building alliances and networks within your industry that focus on DEIB is essential. Beyond the workplace, I can make a positive impact by engaging with my community and by volunteering with DEIB-focused nonprofit organizations and grassroots movements. Joining and supporting organizations dedicated to these values provides opportunities for learning, collaboration, and shared initiatives that can amplify the impact of individual and community efforts. I learned about an organization called GLSEN and began volunteering for them when I was running for a school board position in 2021. When my election concluded, I continued my advocacy efforts by joining the GLSEN Kansas Chapter Board.

Staying informed about the latest DEIB trends, research, and best practices is crucial for individuals and industry professionals. I have brought fresh ideas to each workplace by staying educated and seeking new perspectives. As a vocal advocate for DEIB and demonstrating inclusive behaviors, I lead by example and inspire others to follow suit. Incorporating the values of Diversity, Equity, Inclusion, and Belonging into a banking career was possible and highly impactful. A banking professional can bridge the gap between values and career by advocating for change within the workplace, engaging with the community, influencing investment practices, building networks, and continuously investing in personal development.

It is a journey that requires persistence. The potential to create positive change in the financial industry and in my community made it a meaningful and fulfilling pursuit for the two decades of my life that I committed to the world of banking. By regularly assessing my professional roles and reflecting on my position's capacity to allow me to promote DEIB effectively, I can determine if there are opportunities for paid work, volunteering, or side projects that more closely align with my values and passions. Reflection and adaptation ensure that I continue to live a life that aligns with my core values, contributing to a more inclusive and equitable world. This means that when the workplace no longer serves me and my purpose, I step away from it, to seek fulfilling work elsewhere.

Equilibrium

Finding balance between the many facets of our lives is more complicated than we like to think. I do not believe that there is one magical thing we can do to make everything suddenly perfect. In my mind, it is like balancing a plate on top of a ball. One movement too far in a single direction will topple the plate, and suddenly there are ceramic shards all over the ground. Years ago, I read a book called *The One Thing* by Gary W. Keller and Jay Papasan. The CEO of my employer at the time was hosting an annual book club, and this book was his recommendation. I found a great deal of the book helpful, especially one section about the ebb and flow of balancing work and life.

According to the book, to fully appreciate what our personal lives had to offer, we were likely to put less effort into our work; and to fully engage with our work lives, we would have to make sacrifices in our personal lives. I sacrificed much of my personal life for years to excel at work. Even when I was home with my family, my mind was still on work. I first began to feel as though I was finding balance between my work and home life when the COVID-19 pandemic created an environment where in-office workers like me began to work remotely. My daily commute evaporated, and I found more time in the morning for myself and greater time in the evening for my family.

Stepping into the kitchen to refill my coffee cup provided opportunities to connect briefly with my spouse and kiddo. When I stepped away from my office for a quick restroom break, my dogs followed me on my short walk down the hallway, happy for pats and scritches. Friends stopped by to join me on my lunch break, bringing a lawn chair to sit outside and enjoy the weather and a brief reprieve. I know that there were unknowns and differences of opinion on how to stay safe during this period. My friendship with a person who had previously been dear to my heart for many years became stunted during the first year of the pandemic.

Small disagreements, distance, and an inability to see eye to eye on subjects inside and outside of the pandemic has led to mutual long-term silence. I believe that our friendship has ended. We may no longer be good for each other, but I care for my friend still. He will always be in my heart, and I wish him happiness. I sometimes wonder if we would still have made it to this point in our friendship if the pandemic had not forced us to examine our relationships with others in relation to the health and well-being of our communities.

When thoughts like these creep in and I begin to feel myself going to a dark place, I try to be intentional in reflecting on the things that I gained during the early days of the pandemic. I remember special moments with my spouse and son, getting to hear my dogs howl at the Monday noon bell, and the extra time I got to spend with my folks while we worked on the restoration of our old house (residing and painting)—socially distanced, of course.

I even felt a greater appreciation for my work teammates during this time, as we had to become intentional in how and when we communicated or connected with each other for our success and for the success of our workplace. My friend Rosa and I would meet weekly via Microsoft Teams video to complete our independent tasks and collaborate when the need arose. This gave me much needed social interaction with a friend and colleague. I did not journal during these days, and I think I may regret that when I am older and want to think back on the experiences (good and bad) that I encountered during those world-changing years. It was a lesson that I learned about the importance of documenting our experiences.

The journey to find balance in life is complex. The COVID-19 pandemic, despite its challenges, brought moments of connection with family, pets, and friends. It also led to the reevaluation of friendships and relationships, and the understanding that not all of them will withstand the test of time. Despite the difficulties, intentionally reflecting on the positive aspects of those years helps me maintain a sense of gratitude for the experiences, both positive and negative, that shaped my life.

life

moments

on a timeline

outstretched

thousands

of memories

memories

hidden

forgotten

left behind

moments

on a timeline

that

preserved

life

Te toca a ti! – It's your turn!

Think about one value that you hold. Don't overthink it! Name the first thing that comes to mind. How does it align with your current lifestyle and career choices? This can help you identify areas where you may want to make changes to align with your values and live more meaningfully.

_____

Draw a circle and divide it into 6 sections, similar to how you'd cut a pie. Label each section an area of life that matters to you like work, relationships, health, hobbies, personal development, finances, etc. Assign a rating from 1 to 10 to each area based on how satisfied you currently feel with that area of your life. Are there areas where you score low? Are there areas where you are too focused, leading to neglect in other areas? Identify the areas you would like to improve or restore balance to.

Chapter 3

Reading the Room (and Yourself, Too)

*Understand and manage emotions
to enhance gladness.*

Imagine a world where your interactions with others flowed seamlessly, where you understood your own emotions with clarity, and where empathy became a universal language of connection. This is the world of emotional intelligence, a world we are about to explore in this chapter.

The idea of emotional intelligence may seem vague, but its effects are tangible and far reaching. It determines our ability to build meaningful relationships, to navigate conflicts with grace, and to harness the power of our emotions to fuel personal and professional success.

In the following pages, we will focus on emotional intelligence—recognizing how it shapes our daily lives, influences our decision-making, and propels us toward our goals.

The Not-Quite Wedding Crashers

I must have been twenty years old at the time, barely a grown-up and newly married. New friends from our new church were getting married and we were invited to the celebration after the ceremony. We were running late but I can no longer recall why. I showed up to the venue with my spouse, he was dressed appropriately for the event; as for me...I was dressed super casually in faded blue jeans, Chucks, and one of my favorite shirts, a hand-me-down Orange Crush T-shirt that belonged to my mom when she was my age.

When Ben and I were newlyweds, he always wore beige khaki slacks with a button-down shirt and no tie, even when he was not at work. I, however, have been a jeans and T-shirt person for as long as I can remember. Attending a wedding reception was, in my then young adult opinion, not sufficient reason to call for a change in the wardrobe. I do not think I had attended any kind of formal event as a young adult, other than my own wedding. I will add here that I showed up to my wedding rehearsal wearing Powerpuff Girl pajamas. To this day I am not certain how my spouse felt about it. Whether he thought about my casual attire and attributed it to me being me, or if my standing out in the crowd of fanciful dresses and suits bothered him.

We walked inside the building, found a table with a couple of vacant chairs, and sat down. We watched as the bride and groom walked out onto the dance floor and began to dance, cradling each other in their arms as they swayed. They both looked so adorable and happy; I wanted to share that moment with them. Leaning over to my spouse, smiling wide, I suggested we join our friends on the dance floor. Resigned, knowing that my eagerness was slow to wane, he took my hand as I led him to where our friends were moving back and forth, first leaning left, then right and back again.

It was not until we made our way to the designated space, arms wrapped around each other, mine on Ben's shoulders, his hands resting loosely upon my hips, that I thought something felt peculiar. I began to look around at the other attendees in their fancy clothes, sitting, waiting patiently. *Oh no!* I thought. We were totally crashing the wedding couple's first dance. I had a momentary panic and then knew what had to happen. I leaned into my spouse and whispered-shouted, "This is the first dance. We have to get out of here." Thankfully, he is not one to get rattled easily.

Closing the distance between us, Ben gave me a quick kiss and then we stepped off the dance floor, moving as invisibly as possible back to the table we had been sitting at before the urge to dance had struck me. The rest of the reception continued without any further faux pas. We were not kicked out and our friends had not approached us after the event to grumble about the obvious wedding blunder. I look back on that memory with embarrassment, and I am glad that my youthful lack of life experience did not ruin the special day for my friends. Sometimes our gladness can come from avoiding disaster caused by our own naiveté or ignorance.

Me, Pollyanna

I am a passionate, dedicated LGBTQIA+ advocate and activist. The journey is not always smooth, and challenges often present themselves. However,

I have found that the Glad Game, a simple yet powerful exercise in cultivating a positive perspective, has been an invaluable tool in my efforts. This simple but transformative practice has not only helped me build emotional resilience but has also sharpened my ability to reframe situations positively, fostering a more optimistic and empathetic outlook when I engage with others in the advocacy space. It involves actively seeking out something genuinely positive in situations that are often gut-wrenchingly negative. In the realm of LGBTQIA+ advocacy, this practice can be particularly meaningful.

Some of the major challenges LGBTQIA+ individuals often meet include persistent discrimination, apathy, and prejudice. Rather than succumbing to despair in the face of such negativity, the Glad Game encourages me as an advocate to remain resilient and continue the important work, even when progress seems slow. To illustrate the power of the Glad Game, let us consider an example: preparing to encounter opposition to LGBTQIA+ rights during a public event. I participated in and spoke at a Pride Never Ends rally in my community on July 1, 2023; the same day that hateful, anti-LGBTQIA+ legislation, including a bill preventing transgender individuals from correcting their gender on Kansas birth certificates, went into effect.

Rallies like this were held all over the state of Kansas, giving our LGBTQIA+ brethren a welcoming space to gather and be their authentic selves. Instead of letting the hate-filled legislative negativity dampen my spirits, I was grateful for the opportunity to engage with my community, to speak out publicly in support of LGBTQIA+ inclusion, and to hear the voices of my friends and community. One way I played the Glad Game that day was to create a poster that said: "What if it all works out?" This activity helped me focus on a positive outcome. I brought markers, poster board, and stickers to encourage other attendees to create posters of their own.

Rallies like this one supply a platform for education, allowing us to share our stories, build empathy, and potentially change the hearts and minds of individuals in attendance. The LGBTQIA+ community has been historically marginalized and oppressed, so embracing a mindset of gratitude can help us find strength in unity. The shared struggle fosters a keen sense of camaraderie and solidarity. This fellowship is something to be genuinely glad about. Our collective resilience and determination can lead to considerable progress in the face of adversity.

The Glad Game not only builds resilience but also sharpens my ability to reframe situations positively, fostering a more optimistic and empathetic outlook. In the world of LGBTQIA+ advocacy, optimism is essential. It is easy to become disheartened by the slow pace of positive change, the persistence of discrimination, and the obstacles that arise. However, adopting a positive perspective allows me to keep moving forward with hope. Embracing optimism also encourages me to find cohorts in unexpected places. When I approach others with positivity, it becomes easier to build bridges and encourage support from unlikely sources. This inclusivity helps advance the cause and break down barriers.

Empathy is essential to advocacy. It is important to understand the experiences of LGBTQIA+ individuals to foster a more accepting society filled with allies and advocates. The Glad Game promotes empathy by encouraging us to see things from the perspectives of those who might not initially support us. It reminds us that everyone has their own struggles, and that fostering understanding can be a powerful tool for change. The Glad Game is a valuable companion in this endeavor, helping me build emotional resilience, keep a positive perspective, and cultivate empathy. By embracing gratitude and seeking out the silver lining in challenging situations, I can find strength in unity, foster optimism, and help create a more inclusive world for all.

As advocates, we must remember that the power of positive intention can be transformative. It allows us to navigate adversity with grace, inspire change through hope, and forge connections that bridge divides. Human rights advocacy and activism is a journey filled with both triumphs and trials, but through the Glad Game, I can continue my commitment to LGBTQIA+ advocacy with unwavering determination and perseverance.

I Am One with The Force

In December 2016, I found myself profoundly moved during an opening day screening of *Rogue One: A Star Wars Story*. With my spouse and son in tow, we ventured to my favorite movie theater, the now closed Downtown Warren. Amidst the anticipation of witnessing another chapter in the *Star Wars* saga, a singular moment captured my heart and left an indelible mark on my soul. I was captivated by Donnie Yen's portrayal of Chirrut Îmwe, a blind spiritual warrior.

Despite not being a Jedi, Chirrut Îmwe's unwavering faith in the Force was encapsulated in his mantra: "I am one with the Force, and the Force is with me." This mantra held immense significance, especially during a pivotal scene where Chirrut Îmwe fearlessly walks into danger, repeating these words with conviction. As I sat in the theater, enveloped by the intensity of the moment, Chirrut Îmwe's mantra echoed through me. Goosebumps rose on my skin, and the world around me faded as if only he and I existed in that space. In that instance, I comprehended the profound power of a mantra—a sacred sound that not only resonates within but also transforms the mind and spirit.

The mantra, "I am one with the Force, and the Force is with me," became a catalyst for my self-introspection. It prompted me to reflect on its broader implications beyond the *Star Wars* universe. This simple yet profound affirmation carried a message of hope, courage, and interconnectedness—a reminder that our beliefs can guide us through adversity and uncertainty. This experience left a lasting mark on my spiritual journey, reinforcing my appreciation for the power of wonder and mindfulness in everyday life. It taught me that mantras, whether ancient or fictional, hold the potential to bring clarity, strength, and resilience when faced with challenges.

Embracing this mantra has since become a cornerstone of my approach to life, guiding me with its message of unity and empowerment. In moments of solitude, particularly during my peaceful morning walks through the neighborhood, I find solace in its rhythm. With each step, I take a deep breath. As I exhale, I utter the words, "I am one with the Force," feeling a sense of connection to something greater than myself. With the next inhalation, I affirm, "and the Force is with me," drawing strength and reassurance from this belief.

Amidst the gripping intensity of the film, a heartwarming and lighthearted moment unfolded as Darth Vader made his grand appearance on screen. My young son, swept up in the excitement of seeing his favorite character brandishing his lightsaber, could not contain his glee and joyously exclaimed to the entire theater, "Look! It's DV!" As a lifelong *Star Wars* enthusiast, I had eagerly sought to pass on my passion for the franchise to my son. Witnessing his unbridled delight filled me with immense pride and nostalgia, underscoring the enduring magic and wonder that *Star Wars* continues to evoke across generations.

As I continue to navigate life's complexities, I carry with me the enduring lesson from that transformative moment in the theater—a reminder that, like Chirrut Îmwe, I am connected to something greater, and through belief and perseverance, I can overcome obstacles with unwavering resolve. This connection to the Force, both within and beyond the cinematic universe, serves as a guiding light in my journey toward personal growth and fulfillment.

That One Time I Insulted Spider-Man

In 2014, I attended San Diego Comic-Con with my dear friend Hannah. We had a wild and wacky long weekend, full of cosplaying and generally nerding out over the geeky pop culture exploding out of every orifice of downtown San Diego, California. The streets were alive with color and excitement as fans from all over the world converged to celebrate their favorite movies, TV shows, comics, and video games. The atmosphere was electric, with everyone in high spirits, reveling in the shared joy of their fandoms.

Hannah and I had meticulously planned our outfits, spending weeks perfecting our costumes. One of my cosplays was April O'Neil, complete with yellow jumpsuit and white boots, while Hannah sported an impressive Donna Noble ensemble, donning a gorgeous white wedding gown from her first episode appearing in *Doctor Who*. We spent hours posing for and taking photos, participating in panels and events, and admiring the creativity of other attendees. The convention center was a labyrinth of booths, each one more enticing than the last, filled with exclusive merchandise, rare collectibles, and once-in-a-lifetime experiences.

While walking around inside the confines of the convention center, Hannah and I encountered an individual in full Spider-Man get-up. Their costume was top-notch, with every detail perfectly replicated—from the web patterns on the suit to the sleek mask that covered his face. Those costumes do not leave much to the imagination, so I could tell the guy was in shape. His physique was impressive, and the way he moved suggested he was comfortable and confident in his role as the friendly neighborhood Spider-Man. I fully intended to compliment him and ask for a photo with him, but instead the words that escaped my lips were, "*Aww*, what a tiny Spider-Man!"

This is where I add that the person in cosplay was not much over five feet, which is shorter than the average height of an adult person who I would expect to see cosplaying as Spider-Man. This assumption is unacceptable and not in the spirit of a true nerd, who should appreciate and celebrate the diversity of the fandom without prejudice. Upon hearing my exclamation, Spider-Man's shoulders slumped a fraction and he dropped his head forward—a noticeably sad reaction. In my embarrassment, I fled the scene, my face burning with shame.

I could not believe I had been so thoughtless and rude. The excitement of the convention pushed the moment from my mind for a while as Hannah and I continued to explore and enjoy the myriad activities and attractions. Later that evening, back at our hotel, Hannah and I were reviewing posts on social media from the day's events. We laughed and reminisced about the highlights of the day, scrolling through countless photos and videos. Suddenly, a headline caught my eye: "Daniel Radcliffe Spotted in Disguise at Comic-Con!"

Intrigued, I clicked on the link and was greeted by a photo of the very same Spider-Man I had insulted earlier. My heart sank as I read the caption: Daniel Radcliffe, the beloved actor who brought *Harry Potter* to life, had been at the Con that day in disguise, enjoying the event like any other fan. Yes, I had told Harry Potter he was tiny. The realization hit me like a ton of bricks. I had inadvertently insulted one of my favorite actors, a person who had brought so much joy and magic into my life through his portrayal of Harry Potter. The irony was too much to bear. I felt a deep sense of regret and wished I could turn back time to apologize and make amends.

Reflecting on the incident, I realized the importance of being mindful of my words and actions. Comic conventions are places where people come together to celebrate their passions and find acceptance in a community that shares their interests. My thoughtless comment had momentarily marred that experience for someone else, and it was a lesson I would not soon forget. From that day forward, I vowed to approach every cosplayer interaction with kindness and respect, celebrating the diversity and creativity that makes the nerd community so special.

hiding in plain sight

trauma scars

its victims uniquely remnants

of painful events

linger obvious

light lines painfully painted across the skin
   less obvious

subtle shifts

in character

pressure

to conform

to hide in plain sight fear of what

others may think if they only knew

we are all [of us]

hurting

Te toca a ti! – It's your turn!

Engage in the Glad Game to cultivate a positive perspective in challenging situations. Whenever you encounter a scenario that might be perceived as negative, challenge yourself to find something genuinely positive about it. Embrace a mindset of gratitude and seek out the silver lining.

Reflect on situations where you have experienced strong emotions or witnessed others going through similar experiences. Instead of solely reframing your own thoughts, take a broader perspective. Consider how those emotions might have impacted others involved. Think about what they might have felt, and why.

Practice understanding the emotional experiences of both you and those around you. This exercise deepens your emotional intelligence by fostering empathy, helping you connect better with others, and making more informed decisions in various social and professional contexts.

Chapter 4

Filling Your Own Cup

*Practice self-care mindfully to enhance
overall gladness and well-being.*

Imagine a life where self-care is not a luxury, but a fundamental necessity, where each moment becomes infused with intention and mindfulness. This is the world of mindful self-care, a world we are about to explore in this chapter.

In the following pages, we will visit the power of mindful self-care, identifying how it can rejuvenate the mind, body, and spirit. It is the art of tuning into your needs, acknowledging your worth, and fostering a sense of well-being that radiates from within.

Our Bodies Know Best

A month after my fortieth birthday I began to experience a severe stabbing pain on the upper left side of my chest and back when I tried to breathe while laying down. The pain went on for several days, through the Thanksgiving holiday and into the week following. It only occurred when I was sleeping, or attempting to sleep, and only when laying on my left side, so I disregarded it as aging pain or a pulled muscle in my back. On the morning of the last day of November, the pain did not dissipate when I got up for the day. Breathing became painful, even while sitting and standing. I mentioned the discomfort to my spouse, who dismissed it as I had done, yet by lunchtime the pain was so unbearable that I called Teladoc for a consultation.

After describing my pain, the doctor became serious and instructed me to disconnect the call and go straight to the emergency room. I thanked him for his suggestion and disconnected the call. It felt like my pain could not be something serious enough for a visit to the ER, so I called my primary care physician for a second opinion. I waited on hold and when the technician answered the phone, I nonchalantly explained my symptoms. They placed me on hold and went to talk with my PCP. It was a very brief hold and then the technician came back on the line and told me, very seriously, that I needed to end the call and head straight to the ER.

I told my spouse that I was going to follow their instructions. I felt embarrassed that I was making a big deal out of something that was not. I emailed my boss to let her know I was leaving for the emergency room and off I went. It was the longest 12 hours of my life. I drove to the ER, checked myself in, and followed a person down the hallway to an empty waiting area behind a curtain. I jokingly sent a text message to my spouse at home that I was going to be forgotten by the staff as I sat so far away from the rest of the patients.

After about 45 minutes with no updates, I started to get a little nervous that I really had been forgotten. A short while later, an attendant came over to complete an X-ray of my chest. Two other patients had been placed with me during that time: a young person with a dog bite on his hand and an older man who had chopped the end of a finger off while chopping vegetables while making his breakfast. It was another two hours before anyone else who worked for the hospital appeared in my area. A doctor stopped by to talk to the kid with the dog bite and I took advantage of this appearance to ask about next steps for me. The doctor appeared confused but told me she would investigate it.

Another hour passed without hearing so much as a peep, so I decided it was time to become the detective. I got up and wandered over to the nurse's station. There was no one there, except the technician who had completed my X-ray, who walked by while I was waiting. I reached out my hand and waved her down. She smiled and asked me to sit in a different waiting area. While in the new waiting area, I visited with half a dozen other patients who had been admitted earlier than me and were still waiting for care. The COVID-19 pandemic had severely impacted staffing, causing a bottleneck in service.

After five hours of waiting, I got back up. I asked a desk attendant who might help me understand what diagnostic testing I would undergo when it was my turn. The lady at the counter sent a doctor, who took me to a curtained room outside the waiting area to complete an EKG. The individual who completed my EKG was barely older than a child; she wore *Grey's Anatomy* brand scrubs. I asked her if she was old enough to conduct the

EKG—I have become that person. She laughed and then admitted to me that she still saw her pediatrician even though she was in her early twenties.

I am glad that I am not very modest, because two people walked in to ask questions during the procedure while I was sitting in a chair, shirtless, with a dozen little electrodes stuck on my chest and all over my torso. After that, I was sent back to wait. Another hour passed with no update. I was starting to get dehydrated, and I was feeling a little hangry; I had not had anything to eat or drink since before 7 a.m. and it was 6 p.m. This was my first visit to an ER as an adult and I was not sure what to expect.

I got up once more to request assistance and was sent to a chair off to the side of the admission desk where a technician told me he was happy to take my blood for testing and to put in an IV in case it was necessary for future tests. I asked him why this part hadn't been done earlier since everyone else in the waiting rooms had IVs, and he sheepishly responded that he had been told I left a short while after I was admitted. Someone told him that I decided to refuse care and I had left.

I wanted to be angry but all I could do was to laugh that the joke I had made when I first sat down in that secluded back room hours earlier was the truth. The technician poked my right arm between the wrist and elbow with a needle and the next thing I remember I was on the floor, unsure how I had gotten there. The technician helped me back up onto the chair; he was kind, and I appreciated his bedside manner. It was at this time that he suggested I call someone to sit with me. I was so weak I could barely hold my phone to my ear as I phoned my spouse. He arrived twenty minutes later, kissed my forehead, and sat down beside me. Then we waited. And waited. And waited some more.

After yet another hour passed, I told my spouse that I was worried about having been forgotten again. I asked my spouse to help disconnect me from the heart monitor and help me up. I shuffled from the room, holding tight to my spouse's arm for support and found a man standing at a computer, logging another patient's data. I asked him to please check on the next steps for me since I had not been assigned a doctor and I had been waiting for eight hours for help. I was assured someone would come to me soon and instructed to head back to where I was waiting.

Within the next hour, a doctor came to talk with me about my X-ray and EKG results; he said he wanted to do an MRI with contrast to get a clearer picture of my heart and lungs. I was taken away by a young kid who got lost twice trying to get us to the MRI room. He was new and had to ask someone for directions on how to get the door between the hallways to open. I chalked this up to just another part of this ER adventure. I had never had an MRI with contrast before. It was the weirdest sensation. After the dye was injected through my IV, I had the most realistic feeling that I was peeing my pants... except I was not. It was over very quickly and then I was taken back to my room to wait for the results. When the next doctor came in to talk with us, I had been in the emergency room for twelve hours; it was close to midnight.

The doctor told me that I had suffered from a pulmonary embolism—they found blood clots in my left lung. He said it was highly likely that I also had blood clots in my legs, and he recommended I schedule an ultrasound with my primary care physician to confirm. I was put on a blood thinner at once and was instructed to stop taking birth control immediately due to that being the culprit of my condition. I primarily took birth control to help with keeping my menstrual cycle normal, so it pained me to learn it resulted in this whole health scare.

Less than a week later I got an ultrasound, where blood clots were discovered in my left leg behind the knee. I was instructed to take blood thinners for the near future, a minimum of six months. Thankfully, the clots dissolved naturally over time, and I was safe to discontinue the blood thinner seven months after I started them. As scary as all of this was, I am glad I listened to my body that morning and called the doctor when the pain lasted beyond bedtime.

Had I ignored my pain and just continued with my life, a part of the clot may have broken away and gone to my heart or brain, ending my life. I am also glad I did not dismiss the second doctor's recommendation to get myself to the ER and that I was persistent while there.

Contemplation and Coffee

Mindfulness is an exercise of being fully engaged in the moment, aware of thoughts, feelings, and physical sensations without distraction or self-judgment. I chose to bring mindfulness into my morning routine by focusing on a simple, yet surprisingly insightful daily activity: drinking my very first cup of morning coffee at the dining room table. This quiet moment alone each morning became a ritual after I was laid off from work in early 2023. It offered me a deeper connection to myself and the day ahead through contemplation and reflection—something I rarely took time for when I previously opted to whisk myself off to work and my kiddo off to school with nary a moment of calm.

Each morning, I prepare my coffee with deliberate care. I pay close attention to every detail—the sound of the water heating, the smell of the freshly ground beans, and the sight of the steam rising from the machine as the mystical concoction slowly descends, drip by drip into the pot. I choose the perfect cup for the morning: the handmade ceramic mug brought home from Mexico as a gift to me by my friend Rosa, or the ceramic mug I picked up with my son at the Museum of Modern

Art (MoMA) gift shop—it resembles the toss-away cups often seen in the hands of New Yorkers as they hastily make their way through the busy streets of Manhattan.

I have since added a new mug into the mix, one that my friend Will gave to me as a token of appreciation for my volunteer efforts with GLSEN. It is a tiny version of the mug Rosa gave to me—and I love it! If you ask my family, they are likely to tell you that I have too many mugs, but I say that's poppycock; one can never have too many mugs.

The dining room table—a wedding gift from my parents over twenty years ago— bathed in the soft glow of the early sun, becomes my sanctuary. The familiar surroundings of the table—with its wooden texture and the view of the privacy fence outside, always occupied by a robin, cardinal, or squirrel—set the stage for a mindful morning experience.

When I sit down at the table with my piping hot cup, I take a moment to breathe deeply, inhaling the rich coffee aroma that fills the air. As I bring the cup to my lips, I feel the warmth radiating through the ceramic. The first sip is a burst of flavor—bitter yet smooth, awakening my senses. I savor each sip, noting the texture and temperature, letting the taste linger on my tongue. During these moments, my mind often wanders to the day ahead. But instead of rushing through these thoughts, I allow myself to contemplate them mindfully. I think about the day I have just completed, recalling the most memorable detail of the day and recording it in my planner that sits to the left of me.

Then I start to ponder the tasks ahead that I need to accomplish, the challenges I might encounter, and the goals I hope to achieve. This time at the dining room table becomes a space for setting intentions and mentally preparing myself for whatever the day may bring. Practicing mindfulness during this daily activity has had a profound impact on my overall well-being. I have noticed that I start my days with a greater sense of calm and clarity. The act of being present, even for just a few minutes each morning, helps me to center myself and approach the day with a positive and focused mindset.

It has also enhanced my appreciation for the simple pleasures in life—like the taste of a good cup of coffee and the peacefulness of a quiet morning, something I rarely experienced in years past as I dashed from here to there, stopping briefly at the nearest Starbucks on the way into work. Incorporating mindfulness into my morning coffee routine has transformed an ordinary activity into a meaningful ritual. It provides a moment of tranquility and introspection, setting a positive tone for the rest of the day. By paying attention to every sensation and detail, I find deeper connection and joy in the present moment.

Lunchtime Reverie

On weekdays when my spouse is working and I am not, I have a practice of making my lunch and taking it outside to eat on the front porch. I tend to eat the same thing for lunch every day: half a honey crisp apple sliced up, a couple of chunks of cheese, and a hard-boiled egg, cut up and sprinkled with garlic salt and a dash of freshly ground pepper. I have a favorite folding chair that I bring outside; it is low to the ground and has neck support so I can lean back, relax, and watch the goings on in my neighborhood with comfort. I purchased the folding chair for our annual journey to Winfield, Kansas for the Walnut Valley Festival and this is a fantastic way for me to find value in it year long.

My front porch faces west, which means the house provides shade that protects me from the sun's rays during the early part of the day, and there is a nice breeze to keep me cool during the summer months. In Kansas, there is always a breeze or a gust of wind, depending on the day; it even rains briefly when one least expects it. Sometimes I listen to an audiobook while sitting outside, munching away on my lunch. Other times, I simply sit and watch nature; the only unwanted interruption is the roar of vehicles speeding along the street, on their way from here to there.

Directly across the street from my house is a large patch of grass, a sidewalk, and the bank of a river. Geese often cross the street throughout the day to snack on the grass in my front lawn. When they bring their babies to my yard in the springtime, I watch with awe and affection; they are my favorite birds (uncommon opinion). I have a deep appreciation for these geese parents who work tirelessly to protect their goslings from all the dangers of the human world. Between reckless drivers throughout the neighborhoods and the various litter splashed across the riverbank, we do not make survival easy for them. But they persist.

Taking a mindful break to sit and observe my surroundings without judgment or distraction brings a sense of peace and grounding. As I savor each bite of my simple yet satisfying meal, I become more attuned to the subtle details around me—the rustle of leaves in the breeze, the scratching of squirrels searching for buried nuts, or the gentle honking of the geese. It feels as though time slows down and I am fully present in the moment, appreciating the small wonders of everyday life. In these quiet moments, I learn about my deep connection to nature and my surroundings.

I realize how much I value these simple experiences and how they provide a sense of stability and contentment. Watching the geese care for their young reminds me of the importance of perseverance and resilience, qualities I aspire to embody in my own life. This mindfulness practice teaches me the value of slowing down and taking time for myself. In our fast-paced world, it is easy to get caught up in the rush of daily responsibilities and overlook the beauty that exists in our immediate environment.

By consciously being available to sit and observe, I nurture a sense of inner calm and gratitude. This experiment of intentional observation helps me cultivate a greater appreciation for the present moment and the simple joys that often go unnoticed. It reinforces the importance of being present and fully engaged in whatever we are doing, whether it is eating lunch, observing nature, or simply breathing. Through this practice, I continue to learn and grow, finding new layers of meaning and fulfillment in the ordinary moments of life.

Volunteerism, a Balancing Act

It wasn't until I was in my forties that I was able to say "no" to a request for my time. When asked to attend a meeting at one of my workplaces about being a Mentor to marginalized youth in our community, I said, "Sign me up!" During business, when a customer asked me to help teach English to non-English speaking community members during the evenings once a week, I replied, "Sure, what day?" When asked to lead the youth group at church, I said, "Absolutely!"

The examples go on and on. I seldom turned down an opportunity to do some good because volunteering aligns with my personal mission and values. I rarely regretted the time I spent participating in improving various aspects of my community, but I did come to bemoan the emotional fatigue that began to wear me down. I still struggle a little with it, but I am better at setting boundaries to protect my limited free time. One of my most memorable volunteering experiences was participating in the annual Equality Day, co-hosted by Equality Kansas and GLSEN Kansas. This event, held at our state capitol, brought together over 200 LGBTQIA+ youth, educators, and community leaders.

We had the unique opportunity to hear from a supportive governor, interact with state legislators, and share youth perspectives on issues that matter to public school students across the state. Standing amongst the crowd, I felt inspired to be part of something much bigger than myself. However, my eagerness to help has often led me to overcommit.

I remember one particularly hectic summer and fall when I juggled multiple volunteer roles. I was advocating for LGBTQIA+ youth, chairing the committee on ministry at my church, and writing for an international online leadership publication, and running for public office (I ran for my district's school board position)—all while maintaining my full-time job.

The constant demand for my time and energy took a toll on my mental and emotional well-being. I began to feel stretched thin, unable to give my best to any one cause. It was then that I realized the importance of setting boundaries. Learning to say no was a turning point for me. It was not easy at first; I felt guilty turning down opportunities to help. But I came to understand that by overcommitting, I was not serving myself or the causes I cared about effectively. Setting limits allowed me to focus on the volunteer activities where I could make the most impact. I became more selective, choosing projects that aligned closely with my passions and where my skills were most needed.

Now when I volunteer, I do so with intention and purpose. I have learned to balance my desire to help with the necessity of self-care. This balance has made my volunteer experiences more fulfilling and sustainable. I have also become an advocate for others in my community, encouraging them to find ways to contribute that are meaningful and manageable within their own lives. If you want to make a meaningful, positive impact while connecting with others in your community, try volunteering. It brings people together, fosters a sense of community, and helps address critical needs. But it is also essential to recognize our limits and prioritize our well-being. By doing so, we can continue to give our best to the causes we care about without burning out.

Volunteering has been a cornerstone of my life, shaping who I am and how I engage with the world. While the journey has not always been easy, it has taught me valuable lessons about balance, boundaries, and the importance of giving with a full heart. For anyone looking to volunteer, I encourage you to find your passion, set your limits, and embrace the joy of making a difference—one step at a time.

Acceptance

while settling into the canvas of my lounge chair

the fabric enveloping me

i spied a young bird

exploring the spring grass

it began to sing, a serenade

in the serenity of this fleeting moment I realized

I no longer mourned

i accepted

Te toca a ti! – It's your turn!

Take a mindful break during the day to simply sit and observe your surroundings without judgment or distraction. How did it feel? What did you learn about yourself?

How might taking time to observe the present moment deepen your appreciation and reveal the simple joys that are often overlooked?

Chapter 5

Kindness as a Superpower

*Cultivate self-compassion as a pathway
to intentional gladness.*

Imagine a world where self-criticism is replaced with self-kindness, where you treat yourself with the same warmth and understanding that you offer to your closest friends. This is the world of self-compassion, a world we are about to explore in this chapter.

Self-compassion is not a sign of weakness; it is an act of strength. It is the ability to hold our own hand in times of need, to embrace our flaws as part of our shared human experiences, and to offer ourselves empathy and support so that we are ready to give it to others.

In the pages that follow, we will explore our understanding of self-compassion and begin to pave the way for greater resilience and well-being.

There's Always Time to Feel

My son ran away when he was seventeen months old. Of course, he did not realize he was running away; he ran off in a place he was familiar with and assumed in his baby brain that I would know where he was going and meet him there. It was the most frightening few minutes of my life. We were at the bookstore, a place we visited every weekend since he was four days old; this was known territory to my munchkin. My spouse and I would get a cup of coffee and then take our little one to the children's department to play and look at books.

When he was little, still too small to walk, my spouse and I would put benches or larger stuffed animals around my son and then watch him play in his makeshift playpen as we perused a magazine or book we found on the walk to our destination. My child began to walk at a year and a half, which is later than most children. His father and I were concerned at the time that he might have a developmental challenge; it turned out, according to the pediatrician, that our baby simply preferred to be held and, therefore, opted for being carried over walking.

On the day of the disappearance, my kiddo and I were on a mommy/baby play day visiting our favorite bookstore while his daddy was at work. I was picking up our mess of books, placing them all back on the bookshelves where they belonged. I set my munchkin on the ground to use both hands to put a particularly tricky book away. I turned away from that child for barely a moment. When I turned back to pick him up from the place on the carpeted floor where he was seated, he was gone. In a panic, I dashed down the aisle and around the corner tracing my steps, wondering where he could have gone.

He had vanished on me like a little ninja. I finished scouring the entire children's department. Frantic, I ran into another area of the bookstore to flag down an employee to help me search for my missing baby. Thankfully, the first person I saw was the store manager, and he immediately got on his walkie-talkie to communicate to his team that my kiddo was gone. As I continued to search, dashing up and down the various aisles of bookshelves, I glimpsed a familiar sight. Off to one side of the store, in the back, sat a stairway to the café. Upon the bottom step sat my little guy. Sitting beside him was a woman, eyes darting from left to right, noticeably in search of a parent to go along with the child happily unaware of the scene unfolding within the four walls of the bookstore.

When my child saw me, his eyes lit up. The incident could not have been more than mere minutes from beginning to end but it had felt so much longer. I scooped him up and fell to the floor, cradling my precious cargo in my trembling arms. I began sobbing while my baby tried to figure out why his mommy was sad. From my kiddo's perspective, he had just accomplished a magnificent deed—he had walked all the way from one place to another and he had done it all without help. I am lucky that my story had a happy ending.

I am glad I had people who cared about my kiddo and who were available to immediately support me. Thankfully, there was no nefarious act in play, simply a child asserting independence during a moment when their caretaker was briefly distracted. Understanding that this terrifying experience could happen again, I took my family to Babies "R" Us the very next day and purchased a backpack shaped as a little brown plush monkey that came with a storage pouch in the back and a tail that doubled as a leash. I have judged parents for using harnesses with their children before this experience, but I no longer judge them. We do what we must to keep our children safe.

Seeking Wisdom Between the Pages

"Growing up is a sham but do it well anyway."

I do not know who said this, but I see it every day hanging from my computer monitor in my home office. It is a reminder that despite the challenges and sometimes the absurdities of adulthood, striving to do our best is what truly counts. Like others in 2020, I transitioned to working from home for several weeks. My home office became my mecca—a sanctuary filled with reminders of who I am and what I value. Surrounding me is mostly nerdy artwork, affirmations, a poster from my fifteen seconds of fame in a commercial for a former workplace, and books. So many books.

I am a reader, but I am also a collector of books; these are two different pastimes. I purchase books to read, but I also pick up books simply because I feel they will bring me joy by seeing them sitting smooshed amongst the other books on my bookshelves. ChatGPT says that to call a personal collection a library, one may have between 100 and 200 books. That is a modest number. Between my spouse and me, we have thousands of books spread throughout the house but primarily located in each of our home offices.

Having worked in a bookstore as a young adult, I was unaware that this unlimited access to books is and should be considered a privilege. These books are not just objects; they are sources of wisdom, comfort, and inspiration. Each one holds a world within its pages, a world I can escape to, learn from, and find solace in. From these books, I draw not just knowledge but affirmations that help shape my daily life. Here are three affirmations that I have developed, inspired by the books that fill my home:

- "I am surrounded by knowledge and wisdom." Each book on my shelf is a testament to the vast array of human thought and lived experiences. By immersing myself in these texts, I am constantly reminded of the wealth of knowledge available to me. This affirmation encourages me to keep learning and growing every day.

- "I am capable of creativity through imagination." The stories within my books ignite my own creativity and imagination. They remind me that I too can create, innovate, and dream. By repeating this affirmation, I tap into the boundless creative energy that resides within me, inspired by the narratives and ideas I encounter in my daily reading.

- "I embrace a journey of personal growth." Many of my books are about personal development, philosophy, and the journey of life. This affirmation reminds me that growing up may sometimes be bogus, but it is a journey worth undertaking with sincere effort and dedication. Each day is an opportunity to gain experience, learn, and become a better version of myself.

To build on these affirmations, I draw from the wisdom found in my books and the morning mantras from my *Affirmators! Morning Mantras* card set. Today's card says, "I will do my best today—no matter what. Even if my best is way, way, way less-than-perfect. Still counts!" Incorporating these affirmations into my daily routine, I read them silently first, then aloud. This resonates deeply with me and reinforces the notion that progress is what truly matters, not perfection.

If I am feeling particularly inspired, I even indulge in a solo 30-second dance party. It is a simple act that fills me with joy and energy, setting a positive tone for the rest of the day. Books are my companions, and the affirmations I derive from them guide my thoughts and actions. They remind me that living a life of intentional gladness is a pursuit worth engaging in with passion and sincerity. The thousands of books that line the shelves of my home are not just a personal collection; they are a testament to a life dedicated to learning, imagination, and growth.

A Quest for Silver Linings

Shortly before Thanksgiving 2023, during a well-earned break from work, I stumbled upon a transformative book called *The Artist's Way* by Julia Cameron. My bookshelves house an eclectic mix of titles—most cherished for their wisdom, others merely for aesthetic appeal. For a reason I cannot understand, this book beckoned to me as more than just a display piece; it held the promise of a profound inner journey. To clarify, I am not one for idle contemplation. Sitting still and reflecting does not come naturally to me. I am a person who takes eager action and is always ready to dive headfirst into new adventures, with my gut feeling leading the way.

My son used to have a weekly appointment that presented an opportunity for me to spend approximately forty-five minutes engaged in an activity of my choosing. I would drop him off, and I would occupy myself with various distractions while waiting in my parked car for his appointment to conclude. On sweltering days or extra chilly evenings, the car became my refuge, where I would toggle between the radio and streaming TV on my phone. But when the weather turned pleasant, my routine became more adventurous. I would pop in headphones and immerse myself in an audiobook while exploring the neighborhood on foot.

Around the same time that I discovered the book, a cozy little coffee shop sprung up near the office where my son's appointments took place—serendipity. I decided this was the perfect opportunity to delve into *The Artist's Way* in earnest. One of the initial "assignments" within the book was to start each day by putting pen to paper—actual pen to actual paper—and write until I filled up three pages completely. I could have taken the easy route, opting for a smaller notebook to expedite this task. But, no—I chose a legal pad. Stream of consciousness writing is my comfort zone, which should have made this task a proverbial walk in the park.

However, the challenge turned out to be my choice of location for completing this daily ritual—our bustling dining room. Focus often proved elusive amid the hubbub of my spouse, my kid, and even our four-legged companions. Day by day, I would sit down with my legal pad and pour my thoughts onto those pages, distractions be darned. It was therapeutic, almost meditative—until Thanksgiving weekend. I was away from home, spending the holiday with family. Disruptions to my routine can have a way of derailing my best intentions, but I managed to complete my three pages on Thanksgiving morning.

I decided to grant myself a pass on that post-feast Friday. This was a mistake. Time has passed quickly since then, and I've yet to reclaim the habit of completing morning pages. The routine allowed me to confront the inner chaos that sometimes disrupts my ability to follow through on commitments. By the time I filled the requisite number of pages, I had often unearthed a positive outlook hidden within life's daily challenges. It astonished me how frequently I learned lessons and identified joys that laid beneath the surface.

I long to revive the practice of morning pages. I discovered that I am better when I confront my unspoken emotions and reflect on the positive things in my life, especially at the start of each day. Nowadays, when I pick up a pen and put it to paper, I identify, if nothing else, the benefit of acknowledging the silver linings, which brings a sense of relief and reassurance.

Sorry, Not Sorry – A Fairy Tale

Once upon a time, in a bustling kingdom known as Corporate Land, there lived a young professional named Holly. Holly was talented, hardworking, and full of dreams. However, despite the accolades and promotions bestowed upon them, Holly harbored a secret—they felt like an imposter in their career in the grand castle. Imposter syndrome, a sinister dragon of doubt, lurked in the shadows of Holly's mind. This dragon whispered to Holly that their accomplishments were mere strokes of good fortune and that one day, the kingdom would see through their façade and uncover their true inadequacies.

One fateful day, Holly was summoned by the King of Corporate Land to take on a new, prestigious role as a department manager. Despite their excitement, the dragon of doubt tightened its grip, making Holly feel unworthy of the title. Every decision Holly made was shrouded in fear, and the professional once again tiptoed through the castle halls, worried about being exposed as a fraud. In meetings with fellow knights and advisors, Holly hesitated to share ideas, fearing they would be dismissed as unworthy. This reluctance stifled their creativity, and the weight of constant self-doubt made it difficult to lead their team effectively. Nights were often sleepless, filled with the dragon's whispers that Holly was not good enough.

However, in this kingdom, there were wise mentors and loyal friends who saw Holly's potential. With their help, Holly began to acknowledge the dragon's presence and sought ways to tame it. The first step was to seek feedback from trusted allies, who provided a mirror for Holly to see their true reflection, one not distorted by doubt. With positive reinforcement and constructive criticism, Holly began to realize that their fears were often unfounded. They started keeping a scroll of achievements, no matter how small, and reflecting on these successes helped to counterbalance the dragon's negative whispers. Sharing feelings with trusted friends created a support network, revealing that others in the kingdom also battled similar dragons.

The dragon of doubt had indeed created obstacles in Holly's career journey. There were missed opportunities to highlight their skills and moments of hesitation in pursuing ambitious quests. Yet, with the support of those special mentors and allies, Holly learned to build resilience. Overcoming imposter syndrome became a journey of self-discovery and growth, each step forward marking a victory against the dragon. Holly's story spread throughout Corporate Land, inspiring others to confront their own dragons of doubt. They realized that acknowledging these feelings was the first step toward vanquishing them. By embracing self-awareness, seeking continuous growth, and recognizing their worth, they could navigate the kingdom's challenges with greater confidence.

As Holly continued to climb the ranks, they never forgot the lessons they learned. They committed to mentoring other young professionals and creating an environment where everyone could collectively combat imposter syndrome. The kingdom flourished as more individuals recognized their true potential and celebrated their achievements. And so, in their career in the grand castle, Holly thrived knowing that they were indeed worthy of their success. With each triumph, the dragon of doubt weakened, and the kingdom of Corporate Land became a place where everyone could live happily ever after (ish), confident in their abilities and united in their pursuit of excellence.

The end.

take time

give me a smile
encourage me
i'll smile in return
i am pretending

i feel my face
reaching for
the smile wrinkles
near my eyes
they are absent
i feel nothing

in this moment
i am exhausted
but I smile

Te toca a ti! – It's your turn!

Create a list of positive affirmations to repeat to yourself each day. Start with three and work up from there. I use a set of cards called Affirmators! Morning Mantras. The card I drew this morning says, "I'll do my best today-—no matter what. Even if my best is way way way less-than-perfect. Still Counts!"

———

Identify your negative self-talk patterns or hurtful things that you say to yourself, and challenge them by replacing them with positive self-talk. When I make a mistake, I can say to myself, "That was a really dumb mistake, I am the worst!" This is an example of negative self-talk. I can turn it into positive self-talk by saying something like, "Ope, I made a mistake but I'm still awesome. I will try my best and do better next time."

Chapter 6

Letting Go & Leaning In

*Embrace acceptance and find gladness
in life's uncertainties.*

Picture a life where you greet each surprise, each disappointment, and each unexpected turn of events with a sense of acceptance and grace. Gracious acceptance is not about passive resignation; it is an active acknowledgment of reality as it unfolds.

It is the art of embracing life's imperfections, uncertainties, and ever-changing landscapes with an open heart and a willingness to find the beauty in the unexpected.

We Don't Deserve Dogs

When I hear the phrase "dogs are man's best friend," I think of a bossy mix breed border collie named Monochromatic Rainbow Dash, also called Dash Dog, or simply Dash. She was a beautiful, intelligent canine and she was indeed my spouse's best friend. Unfortunately, she also had special needs. Our healthy, happy Dash Dog was diagnosed with late-onset epilepsy shortly after she turned 3 years old. Her first bout of seizures occurred one sweltering summer evening after we had gone to bed.

Dash usually slept in bed with my spouse and me each night, finding a place at the edge of the mattress to curl up near my spouse's legs. We awoke when our dear pooch fell off the mattress and began convulsing on the hardwood floor of the bedroom. My spouse and I leapt out of bed and went to investigate. I knew what was happening as soon as I saw her little furry body shaking uncontrollably on the ground. I had previously employed a young lady with epilepsy, and she had on more than one occasion fallen victim to seizures in the workplace. I protected Dash's head while my spouse kept our other two curious doggie onlookers away from their seizing sister.

After the seizure concluded, Dash leapt up and shuffled back and forth between the bedroom and bathroom, moving like a zombie as if she were compelled forward by an unknown force. When her overabundance of nervous energy subsided, we settled back into bed and tried to go back to sleep. Less than an hour later, Dash began to seize again. The entire process was repeated two more times. After the third set of seizures, I woke up my son while my spouse cleaned up Dash and carried her, frightened and confused, down the stairs.

We took our dog to the emergency vet hospital where she had more seizure activity under supervision. They kept her at the facility so that they could continue to monitor her and provide medical treatment if necessary. It was after 3 a.m. when we finally made it back home and closer to 4 a.m. when we made our way back to bed. I wish we could have slept in, but we were awake again less than four hours later so I could make it to church in time to be the service leader for the day. I was emotional and exhausted and did not do an excellent job leading the Sunday service, but I did the best I could do under the circumstances.

I'd like to say that this was the first and only time our pooch had seizures, but the following three years were riddled with severe seizure activity, dozens of daily medications, bloodwork, labs, two surgeries after falling outside during a seizure (one broken canine and a follow-up surgery due to infection) and a couple of trips to the School of Veterinary Medicine & Biomedical Sciences in College Station, Texas, eight hours from home. My spouse's heart broke over and over watching his sweet girl suffer from the nightmare that is epilepsy. My son had to get stitches on his finger after he was bitten while helping to protect Dash's head during one of her particularly violent epileptic episodes.

We spent thousands of dollars doing our best to help find a successful treatment program for Dash, but never did get the seizure activity to cease for longer than one to three months at a time. Through all this, Dash never stopped being a happy girl; but over time she became less lucid due to the increasing number of medications intended to keep her seizure-free. After three years and multiple painful conversations between ourselves and the vet clinic, we made the difficult decision to help our six-year-old dog with epilepsy find peace. It may be difficult to see how I can be glad for any of this, especially in 2021 during the continued suffering of our communities due to the ongoing COVID-19 pandemic.

I am not glad for the grief or for Dash's suffering, but I am so glad that Dash came into our lives, showed us love, and that we got to love her and take care of her in return. And thank goodness we were able to afford the specialized care that she required. My friend Rosa pointed out that if Dash had come to a different family, she may not have had the opportunity to live such a long, love-filled life. Six years may not seem like a long time, but Dasher surpassed her original life expectancy after diagnosis by a year. For that reason, and the others I mentioned before, I am glad.

There is a cherry that goes on top of this gladness sundae. One Saturday afternoon, two or three weeks after our Dash Dog passed over the rainbow bridge, my family was lounging at home. I was resting in the living room recovering from a summer cold (thankfully my COVID-19 test had come back negative), my spouse was in his office working, and our kiddo was upstairs watching TV. My spouse came in to suggest we go outside for a little bit to get me out of the house and breathe fresh air. This was an uncharacteristic move on his part; normally I drag him outside for a break. I acquiesced.

I picked myself up off the sofa, still feeling a bit weak and post-feverish. We stepped outside and as we were milling about in the front yard, my parents drove up for a surprise check-in visit. As we were visiting in the driveway, an Animal Services van parked in front of our house. I momentarily panicked, worrying that a neighbor called the city on our older dog that sometimes gets too excitable and barks through the fence at people passing by. A man stepped out of the van and strolled over to our next-door neighbor's house.

He reappeared from around the corner cradling the skinniest little white bag of bones I had ever seen. I rushed over to the man and the words, "We can take care of that puppy!" sprung from my lips before I even registered that I said them. The animal services officer looked down at the puppy in his arms. "I do not know if this little pup is going to make it," he replied to me in a somber tone. "She is starving and severely dehydrated. The neighbor found it in hiding out in his garage; it was probably abandoned."

With his free hand, he pulled a business card from his uniform's shirt pocket and passed it to me, suggesting I call him to find out what rescue accepts the puppy if it survives treatment at the emergency vet clinic. He was on his way straight there. I was instantly in love with the puppy from the moment I laid eyes on her. She could not have been more than ten or fifteen pounds, and that weight was all bones. After the man left with the pooch, I turned to my spouse and begged him to let us adopt her.

He brushed off my request, we finished our conversation with my folks, and headed back inside. I called the officer the next day and he let me know that a local rescue team, Beauties and Beasts, had agreed to take in the puppy. I did not think about the situation for a couple of days and my spouse was the one to bring it up next. He had gone to the rescue website and saw that they were posting information about how the dog was doing at the emergency vet clinic.

She was so little and so weak that they were cautious about being optimistic. He mentioned that we could find out more information about her. I messaged the group and told them we wanted the dog and would love to apply to adopt her. After submitting the application, the rescue reached out to let us know that the vet clinic confirmed the puppy was deaf and they wanted to know if we still wanted to pursue adoption. My spouse and I discussed bringing another special needs dog into our home and agreed that finding out this information did not change the fact that we believed she belonged with us. It took two weeks of intensive care at the emergency vet clinic for the puppy to be well enough to be released.

We had assumed she was just a baby based on her size when we saw her that day on our front lawn, but it turned out she already had her adult teeth, meaning she was closer to six months old. She was categorized as a bull terrier mix, which should have put her around fifty pounds at her age. Instead, she came to us weighing barely eleven pounds. One month after losing our beloved Dash, our hearts began to heal by pouring our love into Alix Kismet Grace, or The Baby. My gladness bucket overflows with ongoing gratitude to my spouse for suggesting we step outside for fresh air on a random Saturday afternoon.

In the beginning, Alix experienced the fear of not getting a next meal; it took us a long while to get her to only eat her food and none from the other dog bowls. Caring for our second special needs dog has had its unique challenges, but they are nothing in comparison to the unconditional love we have received from our sweet deaf baby.

Ein Bisschen Ist besser Als Nichts

My son took German for his language credit in high school. Being the type of person who wants to make sure I can help my kiddo when he asks for it, I decided to also learn German. Before the school semester began, I downloaded the Duolingo app, completed the sign-up requirements, and selected my language. I am also the type of person who learns better when a task is gamified, so the points and sounds indicating success did their job to positively reinforce my daily completion of each German lesson.

At first, it felt like a game I could win with just a bit of effort every day. The streak counter motivated me to log in daily, and the playful nature of the app made it easy to stay engaged. However, I have come to the realization that learning a new language as an adult comes with unique challenges. Unlike children, who absorb new skills effortlessly, I must be more intentional about my learning strategies. Pronunciation has proved especially tricky. German's guttural sounds and the umlauted vowels often feel foreign in my mouth. I get an error sound from the app when I am practicing a speaking exercise and smile while I speak. Funnily enough, I always get it right on the first try when I am frowning.

The most rewarding aspect of this journey in the beginning was the opportunity to bond with my son over our shared struggles and triumphs. I had hoped we might practice speaking together, but he did not sign up for German class in his second year of high school. While my teenager focused on other coursework, I continued my daily ritual of completing a German lesson through the Duolingo app. I find that once I begin a routine, I can keep it going; but I must not lose consistency. It always helps when the task is enjoyable.

I have begun to discover the joy of understanding German culture through its language. The phrases, expressions, and even the structure of sentences give me insight into how Germans think and communicate. Despite the hurdles, I have found that learning German has been immensely rewarding. It has expanded my cognitive abilities and opened me up to a new world of music and cinema. I enjoy listening to German spoken in a film and finding that I understand what is being communicated. The first time I realized I understood what I was hearing in another language was during a rewatch of *Indiana Jones and the Last Crusade*. It was fantastic!

My journey with the German language has been about more than just helping my son. It has become a personal challenge that has enriched my life in unexpected ways. It reminds me that learning is a lifelong process, and that stepping out of my comfort zone can lead to personal growth. When my friend Melanie (who hails from Germany) had friends visit her over a summer, I had the opportunity to chat with them over coffee. I understood parts of what they said (which is better than nothing) and I was even able to respond in small sentences to them in German. *Es war sehr aufregend für mich!*

As I draft this essay, I have completed seven hundred consecutive days of German lessons; every little milestone is a testament to my perseverance and curiosity. Who knows, one day I could be fluent enough to travel to Germany and converse with the locals with ease and confidence. #GOALS!

Glad To Be Here

At a conference I once attended for credit union contact centers, I saw a keynote presentation by John Foley, a former Lead Solo Pilot for the Blue Angels. I searched for longer than I care to admit, attempting to find the photo I had taken with him and to confirm the location of the conference (keep notes, kids; you will not remember everything you would like to). John Foley's career is marked by his exceptional flying skills and his dedication to a unique philosophy he developed and championed called #GladToBeHere.

In my life, I have often said, "I'm glad you're here." It just feels good to be glad.

This philosophy, grounded in gratitude and positivity, has proven transformative for service and team dynamics. Foley's #GladToBeHere philosophy significantly improves service and teamwork by fostering a culture of gratitude, commitment, and excellence. Foley spoke of his time with the Blue Angels and the power of discipline, precision, and teamwork. As Lead Solo Pilot, his performances demonstrated maneuvers that required absolute trust and synchronization with his team.

Through these experiences, he recognized the critical importance of mental and emotional alignment within high-performing teams. This realization led to the creation of the #GladToBeHere philosophy, emphasizing the value of gratitude, mindfulness, and a positive mindset in achieving peak performance. By focusing on what we are thankful for, we can shift our mindset toward positivity and resilience. Foley's philosophy is rooted in the practice of expressing gratitude and being fully present in each moment.

This approach encourages individuals to appreciate their current circumstances and foster a culture where positivity and high performance thrive. I connected with this philosophy because it closely matches my personal focus on intentional gladness. One of the most significant impacts of the #GladToBeHere philosophy is its ability to enhance customer service. By fostering a culture of gratitude, organizations can create more positive and meaningful interactions with their customers. Employees who adopt this mindset are more likely to engage with customers genuinely and empathetically, leading to stronger relationships and improved satisfaction.

I teach my employees that it is important to thank our customers for their time instead of blanketly apologizing when there has been any kind of wait. The simple act of expressing gratitude can transform transactional interactions into positive, memorable experiences that reinforce customer trust and engagement. The influence of #GladToBeHere extends beyond customer service to the core of team dynamics. By encouraging a culture of excellence, Foley's philosophy helps build teams that are not only high-performing, but also deeply connected.

The emphasis on gratitude and positivity fosters collaboration, trust, and mutual respect among team members. This environment nurtures resilience, allowing teams to authentically navigate challenges and setbacks with a growth mindset. Reflecting on the #GladToBeHere philosophy, I find similarities with my personal mission to improve the lives of those around me and my community. The principles of gratitude and positivity align seamlessly with my values and aspirations. Integrating this philosophy into my work and personal projects offers a pathway to fostering a more supportive and thriving environment. By embracing gratitude, I can enhance my leadership style, positively impact my team, and contribute to a more connected and resilient community.

The Day of the Doctor

I am something of a Whovian; that is to say, I love all things *Doctor Who*. I first began to watch the British television show a couple of years after the newly reimagined Ninth Doctor came into being. I could watch episodes on Netflix, which was the only streaming service my family subscribed to pre-pandemic. I binged on all the Ninth Doctor adventures, never having seen the Classic *Doctor*

Who. Sometime shortly after the Doctor had regenerated, my son, who was around kindergarten age, joined me on the sofa to devour as much of the show as we could before it was removed from the streaming service.

We were riveted by the storylines, and quickly found ourselves engulfed in the Whoniverse. We continued to follow the stories as if we were keeping up with faraway friendships. The Tenth Doctor became the Eleventh Doctor, and we mourned the loss of the one who did not want to go while celebrating the one who had arrived to take his place. In November 2013, my friend Aimee and I took my kiddo on a road trip to a small Doctor Who convention in Kansas City, Missouri. We dressed up in themed cosplay; I as the Eleventh Doctor (my favorite), and my son as one of Eleven's companions. We won the cosplay contest, which was exciting, more for me than my son but he was a good sport about it.

The organizers of the event had arranged to play the 50th Anniversary Doctor Who Special live in the theater located on-premises. The anniversary episode was the length of a movie, and delivered all the excitement, humor, and drama that we had come to expect from any *Doctor Who* episode. I have a framed caricature from this event hanging in my house. Whenever I walk past it, the Sharpie-drawn smiles on our cartoonish faces bring a genuine smile to my lips. Later that evening, while still in our cosplays, we visited my brother on the set of a film he was creating. The scene they were working on when we arrived took place in a hospital lobby. My brother fed us pizza on set and then asked if we would like to sit in as extras in the scene. It was exciting to be a part of something my brother was creating—he is an incredibly talented industry professional.

We sat on the set of a hospital lobby, no longer looking like we were from a Doctor Who convention, but our outfits still very much stood out. My favorite part of the experience was when they had to keep cutting the scene because the camera person could catch my kid in the background (where we were seated) quoting the lines as the actors were saying them. It was hilarious (for me) but unnerving for the hard-working crew. After hugging my brother goodbye and saying our farewells to our friends on set, we embarked on the final adventure of the night: making our way to the hotel. I finally had a smart phone with GPS capabilities which helped reduce travel time.

We got one more good laugh in for the evening as the hotel front desk attendant complimented my friend and I on our adorable family. I remember simply thanking the person for the compliment, but we had a good laugh about it once we made our way to the room. Although this event occurred over a decade ago, it stands out as a treasured memory. Aimee and I talk about it occasionally, and together we can recall the day's events—I am not certain that I could do it all on my own. My son does not recall much of the experience but that hardly stops me from attempting to remind him of the fun he had playing pretend.

an ode

my heart it

aches

inside my chest

surges

of adrenaline flowing

nature's way of

alerting

love

every fiber of my being a

xylophone's symphony of

acceptance

never enough time to

devote you are for-

ever my

reason

Te toca a ti! – It's your turn!

Commit to 10 days of guided support focused on a topic of personal development that interests you. Choose from activities such as journaling, meditation, exercise, gratitude, gardening, or any other area you wish to explore or improve. After completing 10 days, challenge yourself to extend your streak by another 10 days.

Chapter 7

The People Who Shape Us

*Explore the impact of positive relationships
on intentional gladness.*

Imagine that your relationships are not just fleeting encounters, but enduring, enriching chapters of your life's story—a world where you cultivate deep connections that thrive and flourish.

Nurturing relationships is not merely about having more friends on social media or acquaintances in your contact list. It is about fostering genuine, meaningful connections that bring joy, support, and a sense of belonging.

Pandemic Lessons in Parenthood and Leadership

I spent the majority of 2020 working from my home office, with my school-aged kiddo down the hallway in class remotely, and my spouse working from the library downstairs. It was both a challenge and a unique opportunity to invest in the lives of others—my teammates and my family—during an extraordinary time in our world. Being a leader is hard work, whether you are parenting your child or guiding your work team through challenges. It is also rewarding, and can bring with it lasting fulfillment. Like parenthood, leadership in the workplace takes time, focus, drive, and passion, and I have found that many of these skills have overlapped.

Our children begin their lives as blank canvases, full of potential. We, the parents, are accountable for shaping these small humans into empathetic, compassionate, responsible adults. We use our experiences to teach our kids to be logical, while also encouraging them to maintain their creativity and sense of humor. While our team members are not blank canvases, they may be new to the field, and we have the same responsibilities to guide them.

We are not perfect, and we may not always demonstrate the love we have in our hearts for those around us, but the love is there. I learn and grow every day as a parent, just as I learn and grow every day as a leader. It would be foolish to say that every decision I made during that time was the right one, but it was the best decision I felt I could make with the information I had at the time. As author Judy Belmont said, "Forgive yourself for not having the foresight to know what now seems so obvious in hindsight."

Here are three important lessons I have learned this past year that have helped me to be a better leader and parent:

Lesson 1: Practice Patience. Maintaining focus for a full school day has been a constant battle for my child. Having to sit in one place all day surrounded by distractions is a challenge for both kids and adults. Similarly, not every one of my teammates felt that they could be productive working from home—whether it was their workspace, having other people in the house during the workday, or a feeling of isolation. Remote work is not for everyone. Although being swift to action benefited me and my team during the early stages of the pandemic, I learned that the same strategies don't work long-term for everyone. I had to slow down to allow others to walk alongside me on the journey, taking time to clarify the plan and genuinely listen to feedback. Though I am not a naturally patient person, I learned that I must practice patience to continue to support both my family and my team.

Lesson 2: Give Grace. I collect coffee mugs. One of my favorite mugs has the phrase "Live Your Kind" on it. It is a reminder to me that kindness is the key to a happy life. It takes very little to be kind, yet it can make all the difference in the world. Accountability in the workplace looks different than it has in the past. Each teammate is working through their own personal struggles due to the pandemic on top of meeting their work expectations. Ensuring that my team has the tools to take care of their mental health is one of my responsibilities, but it evolved to become more of a team effort and less of an individual focus. We look out for each other and build each other up by sharing our vulnerabilities. Through this kindness, we show that we are all human and we are all in this together.

Lesson 3: Be Okay with Where You Are Now. There have been times when I have urged my child to grow up and attempt to be as responsible as the adults I work with each day. But when I observed that my kiddo needed to simply be a kid, I stepped back and gave him room to play and a safe place to fail. When my teammates have become overwhelmed at work or at home, they are encouraged to find ways to de-stress and rejuvenate. Our team continues to find ways to bring joy and frivolity into the workplace and celebrate each other.

The lessons I have learned do not make me a picture-perfect parent or a flawless leader, but they have helped me gain a better grasp of the human elements of parenthood that are helpful in leadership too. I recognize the joys and sorrows of being responsible for others, and I firmly believe that understanding and appreciating ourselves allows us to do the same for those in our care. I try to remember that we have all had things go wrong and had to reach out for help. When we are desperate, we just want to feel like someone is on our side. Be on the side of your team.

The Art of Keeping in Touch

I am notoriously bad at staying in touch with people in my life if our paths do not regularly intersect. Growing up, frequent moves meant leaving behind best friends with each relocation. Initially, I tried to maintain contact, but inevitably, the connections faded due to my tendency to focus only on what—and who—was immediately in front of me. As an adult, my closest friendships often stem from shared workplaces or volunteer commitments. Some of these friendships trace back to my early twenties, where bonds formed and then drifted apart, only to be rekindled unexpectedly in my thirties. These reconnections have been a source of immense gratitude, enriching my life with enduring relationships.

Social media has become my tool for intermittent connection, offering glimpses into the lives of distant friends. Yet I have come to realize that these platforms often showcase curated highlights, leaving me unaware of the challenges and hardships they may face. I have been absent during their darker moments, which cannot be shared as readily online. What strikes me is how profoundly I cherish moments of sustained connection—whether through a friend visiting town or a heartfelt exchange via text or email. These interactions fill me with joy and deepen my sense of fulfillment in relationships.

To nurture these connections, I have found that bringing my friends together can be incredibly rewarding. When my various circles of friends get to know and appreciate each other, it strengthens the overall network of relationships in my life. It creates a sense of community where everyone feels connected, and it often leads to new shared experiences and memories. However, this approach also comes with its challenges. I sometimes find myself grappling with FOMO (the fear of missing out), especially when my friends make plans without me or if I am invited to participate in an activity but unable to for one reason or another.

While I understand that it is natural for people to have their own social interactions, I cannot help but feel a twinge of irrational disappointment when I am not included. It is a reminder of my desire to be actively involved and valued in the lives of those I care about. It is also a reminder that I am only the main character in my story. Reflecting on these dynamics, I realize that maintaining friendships requires both effort and acceptance. It is about finding a balance between nurturing individual connections and fostering a broader sense of community. This balance allows me to appreciate the unique strengths and joys that each friendship brings, while also acknowledging the occasional challenges that come with distance and differing schedules.

Looking ahead, I aspire to cultivate deeper connections by being more proactive in reaching out and staying engaged. Whether through regular check-ins, shared activities, or simply being present in both good times and bad, I hope to strengthen the bonds that enrich my life. By embracing the complexities of friendship and opportunities for growth that each unique relationship offers, I aim to continue learning and evolving in my journey of connection and reconnection.

Active Listening and the ADHD Brain

I once saw a video on social media that perfectly illustrated what happens in an ADHD brain when it is time to go to sleep. Imagine a never-ending medley of overlapping songs, all blending into a chaotic yet somehow harmonious montage. This is exactly what happens to my brain during a conversation when I am not being intentional about active listening. If my body is not physically moving, you can bet that inside, my brain is throwing one heck of a rager.

Active listening is a skill I have had to consciously develop, much like learning to DJ at my brain's internal rave. Without it, my thoughts spin like vinyl records on turntables, remixing random ideas and snippets of conversation into a mental techno dance party. As a result, my focus on the speaker often wavers, replaced by an internal monologue contemplating everything from the meaning of life [42!] to what I will have for dinner (probably a gluten-free bagel with cream cheese).

The challenge lies in quieting this mental rave long enough to truly engage with the person I am listening to. It is not just about hearing their words; it is about immersing myself in their story, asking questions, and providing feedback that shows I value and respect their opinions. Active listening is like being the ultimate dance partner—moving in sync with the speaker's rhythm, matching their pace, and responding to their cues.

Imagine sitting across from someone who is sharing a heartfelt story. They are pouring their emotions into their words, and you are trying your best to stay present. Suddenly, a rogue thought crashes the party: *Did I remember to unplug the griddle?* Before you know it, you are deep into a mental checklist of errands and chores, miles away from the conversation at hand. This is where the practice of active listening comes into play.

The first thing I must do when these moments arise is to acknowledge the distraction. Instead of letting it spiral, I take a deep breath and mentally note, *Okay, that's a rogue thought.* Then, I gently guide my focus back to the speaker, much like a DJ transitioning from one song to the next without skipping a beat.

Next, I engage the other person through curiosity. Asking questions is my secret weapon. Not only does it show the speaker that I am genuinely interested, but it also helps anchor my attention to the present moment. "Can you tell me more about that?" or, "How did that go for you?" are my go-to questions that encourage deeper connection and understanding.

Lastly, I provide feedback. Nodding, maintaining eye contact, and offering verbal affirmations like, "I see," or, "That sounds tough," are small yet powerful ways to show empathy and engagement. It is like being the hype person at a concert, amplifying the energy and validating the speaker's experience.

When I get excited and want to show that I am engaged in a conversation, I sometimes inadvertently interrupt the speaker before they have finished expressing their thoughts. While my interruptions are well-intentioned, I realize they can be distracting. I have also learned that maintaining eye contact is crucial for active listening [for me]; when I lose eye contact, I recognize that I am no longer fully attentive to the speaker.

Despite the rave in my brain, I have learned that active listening is a dance worth mastering. It is a practice that requires patience, mindfulness, and a genuine desire to connect with others. By quieting the mental DJ and tuning into the rhythm of the conversation, I can transform my internal chaos into a harmonious exchange of ideas and emotions.

In a world where distractions are constant and attention spans are shrinking, active listening stands out as a superpower. It shows others that we value their words, respect their opinions, and are present in the moment with them. The next time you find yourself in a conversation, remember to turn down the volume on your mental rock show and tune to the speaker's frequency. You might just discover a new level of connection and understanding that turns an ordinary chat into an extraordinary dance of minds.

Birthday Parties: The Ultimate Team Building Adventure

One of my favorite traditions each year is bringing as many of my friends together as I can to celebrate my birthday on October 19 (at 10:19!). I have been practicing this ritual for over twenty years, and every part of it—from planning, to rallying my friends, to executing my birthday shenanigans—brings me great joy. I often start planning my birthday adventure sometime between my un-birthday (April 19) and the summertime with a "save the date" text to my friends and loved ones. As the date approaches, I send individual check-in messages to gauge everyone's RSVP status. Over the years, I have had as few as a handful to as many as two dozen attendees, which always feels like a big deal to me.

In my twenties, my grown-up birthday parties often took place at hibachi restaurants. The simplicity of reserving a table and the familiarity of the experience made it an easy choice. However, as I entered my thirties, I decided to focus on fun and frivolity. For instance, my city has a science center that hosts all sorts of super cool grown-up activities, including zombie-themed evenings with finger foods, science experiments, and eerie activity rooms filled with zombies.

During the height of the COVID-19 pandemic, I was not sure how to celebrate my birthday. I knew that I desperately wanted to see my friends, many of whom I had not seen in ages due to safety protocols and quarantines in my city. I found a local pizzeria willing to rent me their outdoor patio area. We arranged four separate picnic tables for guests to come and go, enjoying pizza and soda. I brought pumpkin pie from home for everyone, making sure to individually package the pie slices for safety.

My forty-first birthday party took place at a dinosaur-themed adventure park in a nearby city. We got to walk around the park in the dark, playing games, trick-or-treating, and channeling our inner ten-year-olds. My friends with kids even dressed their little ones in Halloween costumes, making it an inclusive event for all ages. My birthday's proximity to Halloween affords me the unique opportunity to hijack Halloween-themed experiences for my celebration. Reflecting on these celebrations, I realize that my birthday parties are more than just fun events—they are a testament to the bonds I share with my friends and loved ones. Each gathering, whether it is a simple dinner or an elaborate themed adventure, strengthens our connections and creates cherished memories.

Over the years, I have learned that the joy of these celebrations lies not in the extravagance of the event, but in the shared laughter, the creativity in planning, and the sense of togetherness that each birthday brings. As I look forward to future celebrations, I am reminded of the importance of these moments. They serve as a reminder that despite the passage of time and the changes life brings, the spirit of camaraderie and the joy of bringing people together remain constant. My birthday parties have truly become the ultimate team-building adventures, celebrating not just another year of my life, but the enduring friendships and love that make each year special.

make believe

running down dark streets at night

dodging cars as they pass by

creeping through yards like we're spies

climbing fences

building tales within our minds

imagining storylines

creating mischief smiles wide

doing normal kid shit

Te toca a ti! – It's your turn!

Practice recognizing and appreciating positive qualities in others. Take the time to genuinely acknowledge someone's strengths, accomplishments, or unique qualities. Share your heartfelt observations with them, highlighting the positive impact they have on you or others.

This exercise not only spreads joy but also enhances your emotional intelligence by honing your ability to empathetically connect with others, fostering positive relationships, and creating a more emotionally supportive environment.

———

When having a conversation, try to focus on the speaker's words and avoid thinking about what you will say next. Ask questions and provide feedback to show that you are engaged and interested in what they have to say. Active listening is a powerful way to show someone that you value and respect their opinions.

Chapter 8

Living Unapologetically

*Foster gladness by embracing
and expressing your true self.*

Imagine being free to express your thoughts, feelings, and aspirations without fear of judgment, where you move through the world guided by your inner compass, and where you recognize that your unique essence is not only enough, but is also your greatest strength.

Embracing authenticity is not merely about "being yourself" in a superficial sense; it is about connecting with the deepest, most genuine parts of who you are and allowing that authenticity to guide your choices, actions, and relationships. It is the art of living in alignment with your true self, unapologetically and authentically.

A Leader's Advice to Their Younger Self

I wrote this article, published at the start of 2023, just a month before I was laid off. In hindsight, it's a powerful reminder that I already had the wisdom I needed to find myself within me—wisdom about leadership, growth, and understanding that my career does not define my identity.

> Dear Me,
>
> Remember the magnet on your fridge? The one with the Oscar Wilde quote: "Life is far too important a thing to ever talk seriously about." While that may be true for life itself, the actual act of taking charge of your life is too important to not talk seriously about. This is also true about your professional life as a contact center leader. You may not realize this just yet, but you are enough.
>
> You are growing in your confidence and have many accomplishments behind you. You are finding out what leadership looks like and feels like to you—and that is the ultimate achievement in a professional journey. You are celebrating your growth

as a leader and the contributions you make. Know this journey is not without its struggles, so to help it be a smoother road, I want to share some advice:

Leadership is not about being the best. It is about helping others be their best. When those you are responsible for shine, you will also shine. In the beginning, you are going to be a rock star performer, and you are going to think being the best is how you create the best. A better way to lead is to learn everything you can about the job, do every aspect of the job you can, and then—as the ultimate leadership achievement—learn how to inspire others to find their own way to succeed in the role. This will be hard at first, but it gets easier as you come to understand that everyone's personal and professional journey is different. Each person will bring their own perspective, experience, and strengths into their work. Your team will be more well-rounded if you focus on developing other people's natural strengths.

Leadership is not about telling others what to do. It is about helping those you lead trust you and walk alongside you. You will want to give advice whenever you think you can save someone time or discomfort from learning a lesson (and you will), but people often learn the most when they try something out for themselves.

Be willing to ask tough questions and be willing to try new (and sometimes scary) things. It is okay to let people learn from their mistakes. In fact, you will become an expert in encouraging others to try things and allowing them to safely fail. If you fail from time to time, do not beat yourself up over it. Learn from your mistakes and commit to being more intentional when you interact with your crew. Consider active listening—there would not be so many learning materials out there targeted toward improving listening if we were all naturally great at it.

Leadership is not about being the same as every other leader. You were not born to be someone else. No matter how much you think it can help you get ahead, trying to be like other leaders in your industry simply comes off as inauthentic. Other leaders will give you well-intentioned advice from time to time, recommending you try to assimilate or replicate how your peers present themselves. Hear them out, but do not let it lead you to question your value. Sure, you can attempt to dress and speak like your peers, but you will feel lacking on the inside because you are not leveraging the genuine, unique leadership characteristics that make you *you*. I know it is easier said than done, but do not worry too much about being different from other professionals. Just be you.

On a lighter note, you will find ways to make work both fulfilling and enjoyable for your team. Yes, it is possible to achieve great things and have fun, too. Do not lose sight of how important this is for those who you lead—your passion in life can generate enthusiasm in others.

Those in positions of power who see you and recognize your potential will be willing to invest their time in your growth. Be warned—you may get impatient, and there will be tough days, but you will be a better leader for having pushed through it all. Nothing—good or bad—lasts forever. I am already so proud of the leader you will become. You are up for the challenge; accept the offer when it comes and continue to work to be a better version of yourself every single day.

With love,

You

P.S. Be sure to find someone (a friend or confidant) who will take the time to tell you it will all be okay when you need to hear it.

Your Mission, Should You Choose to Accept It

Life is a continuous journey of growth and self-discovery shaped by our experiences, values, and goals. Reflecting on my life journey has been a profound exercise in understanding the patterns and themes that define who I am and what I aspire to achieve. Several patterns and themes emerge, but one consistent thread throughout my life is a deep-seated desire to make a meaningful difference in the lives of those around me. Through this reflection, I have crafted a personal mission statement that encapsulates my core values, passions, and aspirations.

> *My mission is to uplift the voices of those around me and help weave a stronger, kinder community wherever I am — a place where people [and animals] feel safe, seen, and supported.*

My life experiences have significantly influenced my values and goals. From personal challenges to professional achievements, each experience has contributed to my understanding of what is truly important. These experiences have highlighted the importance of compassion, community engagement, and personal development. I remember going to my first demonstration as a young college student with a few friends of mine from the local Unitarian Universalist church. I made two signs and attached them to a yardstick to carry them both together. On one sign, I painted a wedding cake and a message about marriage equality. On the other sign, I painted the words: "Love is Love."

Somewhere I have a picture of 2005-me holding the signs up in front of the Kansas Capitol Building, my nose a bright red, matching the heavy winter coat I wore to defend me from the chill of the freezing January wind. This was not only my first human rights demonstration, but also the first time I took time off work to participate in an equal rights event. Whether through professional endeavors, volunteer work, or personal relationships, my actions have been driven by a commitment to improving the well-being of others and fostering a sense of community. As a white person, I live with a certain level of privilege; I believe that it is my civic responsibility to use my voice to help uplift others who experience marginalization.

The recurring theme of community service and support has shaped my goals and aspirations. I have seen firsthand how collective effort and genuine care can lead to positive change, reinforcing my belief in the importance of contributing to the greater good. I am committed to fostering compassion, believing that through empathy and proactive engagement, we can build more supportive and thriving environments for all. This mission serves as a guiding principle for my actions and decisions, aligning my daily efforts with my overarching goal of making a positive impact. By embracing this mission, I am guided by a clear sense of purpose, which shapes my actions and decisions, ensuring that I remain committed to improving the lives of others and my community.

In a World Where...

My commitment to human rights stands as the beacon of hope and change while disparities and injustices are still widespread. The impact I wish to make in the world can often be traced back to understanding that we all deserve human dignity and equality. For those dedicated to this cause, the journey toward making a tangible difference begins with recognizing our unique skills and talents, and then leveraging these to explore new activities and avenues that align with our interests and values.

Every individual possesses a distinct set of skills and talents that can significantly contribute to the cause of human rights. Whether it is a knack for persuasive communication, an analytical mind adept at understanding complex legal frameworks, or an empathetic approach to community engagement, these abilities can be powerful tools in the fight for justice. Identifying these strengths is the first step toward understanding how one can best contribute to the broader goal of human rights advocacy.

For those with a legal background, working in human rights law offers a direct avenue to impact. Lawyers can represent marginalized individuals, challenge unjust laws, and work on policy reform. Nonprofit organizations, international bodies like the United Nations, and government agencies are often in need of legal expertise to navigate the complexities of human rights legislation and enforcement. Journalists and media professionals play a critical role in bringing human rights issues to light. Investigative reporting can uncover injustices and give a voice to the voiceless. By crafting compelling narratives, journalists can educate the public, influence opinion, and advocate for change. This requires not only excellent storytelling skills, but also a deep understanding of the issues at hand.

Educators and trainers have the power to shape the next generation's understanding of human rights. By developing curricula that highlight the importance of human rights, teaching in schools, or running community workshops, educators can foster a culture of empathy and activism. This grassroots approach can create a ripple effect, empowering individuals to advocate for not only their own rights, but those of others.

Activists working at the grassroots level often serve as the frontline defenders of human rights. Organizing protests, creating community programs, and engaging in direct action can put pressure on authorities to address injustices. This requires strong organizational skills, the ability to mobilize and inspire others, and a deep commitment to the cause. In the digital age, technology offers new tools for human rights advocacy. From developing apps that document abuses, to using data analytics to track and predict human rights violations, tech-savvy individuals can make substantial contributions. This field requires both technical expertise and creative problem-solving to develop innovative solutions that can be scaled globally.

Trying new activities and hobbies that align with your interests and values can open up unexpected opportunities to contribute to human rights causes. Here are four examples:

- Volunteering: Engaging with local human rights organizations can provide practical experience and insights into the challenges and opportunities in the field.

- Writing and Blogging: Sharing thoughts and experiences related to human rights through writing can raise awareness and inspire others to take action.

- Public Speaking: Developing skills in public speaking can amplify one's voice and influence, allowing them to advocate effectively in various forums.

- Networking: Building connections with other advocates, attending conferences, and participating in online forums can lead to collaborations and inspire new initiatives.

- Buying Power: How you spend your money reveals a great deal about your values and beliefs. It's not just about your purchases; it's a reflection of what truly matters to you in life.

Embarking on a journey to improve the world through human rights advocacy is both challenging and rewarding. It requires a steadfast commitment to learning, adapting, and growing. By understanding one's unique skills and talents and exploring new activities that align with their mission, individuals can find their place in the broader human rights movement. The impact one wishes to make in the world reflects one's dedication to the principles of justice, equality, and dignity. We can contribute meaningfully to the ongoing fight for human rights and make the world a better place for all by actively seeking opportunities to apply our unique strengths and explore new avenues for engagement.

We All Have the Power to Name Ourselves

When I was about six years old, my closest friends and I would pretend that we were Teenage Mutant Ninja Turtles. I was the only kid who was not a boy, so my friends David, Michael, and Jeff, always tried to get me to pretend to be April O'Neil, the strong, curious, independent best friend of the turtles. Although I love April and acknowledge that she is my first fictional feminist role model, I always wanted to play Michelangelo—our personalities and identities were so much more in sync. Michelangelo's carefree, fun-loving nature resonated with me, and I felt an unspoken kinship with his character that went beyond just admiration.

Fast forward a few decades. I am sitting in my therapist's office, and she asks me a question about my emotional triggers related to anti-LGBTQIA+ legislation and my individual identity. I cannot recall the exact question. I only remember that my response was automatic: "Oh, my gosh! I'm nonbinary." Until this moment, I never voiced aloud that I have always felt a little like I cosplay my gender assigned at birth; I have never felt like female was the right word to describe my gender. The realization was both liberating and startling.

How could I have overlooked such an important aspect of my personal identity?

I started to reflect on all the times throughout my life when I felt out of place, like I was wearing an ill-fitting costume. From the discomfort of wearing traditionally feminine clothing, to the awkwardness of being referred to with she/her pronouns, I began to see a pattern. Growing up, there were subtle signs that my gender identity did not align with societal expectations. I remember feeling a sense of envy when my male friends could express themselves freely without the constraints of gender norms. I often felt a disconnect between how society expected me to behave and how I truly felt inside.

Looking back again on my childhood, even when I played pretend by myself, I did not play a feminine character; I would pretend to be a gritty detective on the search for some missing dame. As an adult, I was introduced to Jessica Jones from the darker side of the Marvel universe. She was much more like the character I portrayed in my youth than the PI from *Who Framed Roger Rabbit*.

As an adult, these feelings never quite went away. I find myself drawn to androgynous fashion, feeling most comfortable in clothes that do not scream "female." I have experimented with different hairstyles—sometimes going for a more traditionally masculine look, other times embracing a somewhat feminine style, but primarily sticking to shorter, gender-neutral styles. It is a constant balancing act, trying to navigate a world that seems to insist on fitting me into one box or another.

Everything clicked into place in that pivotal moment in my therapist's office. I finally understood why I had always felt like an outsider, even in spaces that were supposed to be inclusive. I realized that my discomfort with traditional gender roles was not just a phase or a quirk; it was a fundamental aspect of who I am. Embracing my nonbinary identity has been a journey of self-discovery and acceptance. It is about unlearning the societal expectations ingrained in me and finding the courage to define my own identity on my terms. Since that revelation, I have explored what it means to live authentically as a gender-nonconforming person.

I have adopted she/they pronouns, finding solace in a label that finally feels closer to accurate. I have connected with others in the LGBTQIA+ community, sharing experiences and finding strength in our collective journey. Each step forward is a step toward living a life that feels true to who I am, free from the constraints of traditional gender norms. It was important for me to share this information with my kiddo and my spouse first. My kiddo was great; he asked me if it was still okay to call me mom (I said yep). My spouse did not appear fazed by my announcement; he only asked me if it changed anything about our relationship (it did not). We talked a little about revised pronouns, and that was that.

My brother's response was also perfect. I can no longer quote his exact response, but it went something like, "Oh yeah, I already knew that." He asked about my pronouns and has been respectful of using them correctly since our conversation. When I took my friend Rosa to lunch to tell her that I am nonbinary, her response was almost identical to my brother's. She affirmed me and added, "Is that it? I thought you were going to tell me some bad news."

I never came out to my parents. I know my folks love me, and they have never made me feel like I wasn't loved and accepted for who I am, but I still struggle with the fear of rejection that I've seen happen to others when they come out to their parents, regardless of their age.

It feels like a dick move coming out in a book—alas—surprise, Mom and Dad! You have a gender-nonconforming kid. I love you!

possibility

why

is it

easier

to help others

embrace

doing

what

is good

for them

yet so difficult

to do

ourselves?

Te toca a ti! – It's your turn!

Reflect on your life experiences and how they have shaped your values and goals. This can help you identify patterns and themes that may be relevant to your "Why." Now, write a personal mission statement that encapsulates your values, passions, and desired impact. This can serve as a guiding principle for your life and decision-making.

Think about the impact you want to make in the world, and how your unique skills and talents could contribute to this goal. Then, try new activities or hobbies that align with your interests and values, to explore new avenues for fulfilling your "Why."

Chapter 9

Bouncing Back

Explore the role of resilience in maintaining gladness amidst challenges.

Imagine a life where, instead of breaking your spirit, adversity becomes a stepping stone to growth, where challenges are opportunities in disguise, and where you possess the unwavering ability to bounce back from setbacks with strength and wisdom.

Resilience is not merely about toughness or the ability to endure; it is the art of adapting and thriving in the face of adversity. It is the inner resource that helps you not only survive, but flourish amidst life's greatest challenges. It is a skill that can be developed, nurtured, and harnessed to overcome obstacles both large and small.

Navigating the Turbulence of Job Loss

Losing a job is often cited as one of the most stressful life events a person can experience. For me, being laid off from the organization to which I had devoted over fifteen years of my life was a profound shock. This was not just a job; it was a place where I had built my career, forged deep relationships, and envisioned staying until retirement. The unexpected severance left me grappling with a whirlwind of emotions, from disbelief and anger, to sadness and fear for the future.

The immediate aftermath of the layoff was marked by a period of intense reflection. I found myself questioning what went wrong and why it happened to me. There were sleepless nights spent replaying scenarios and wondering if I could have done something differently. This process of reflection, although painful, was crucial in helping me understand that the layoff was not a reflection of my worth or capabilities, but rather a result of broader organizational changes and economic factors.

The emotional toll of losing a long-term job can be compared to other significant life stressors, such as the death of a loved one, divorce, or a major illness. The stability and identity tied to my role at the organization were abruptly taken away, replaced by feelings of grief and a loss of purpose. To cope, I began to consciously shift my language from one of defeat to one of resilience. Instead of saying, "I'm worthless," I started telling myself, "I have value, and I will find a new path." This subtle change in self-talk reinforced the notion that this setback could be a catalyst for personal growth and new opportunities.

One of the most important steps in my healing process was seeking support from friends, family, and professionals. Sharing my experience with trusted individuals provided a sense of validation and relief. It was comforting to know that I was not alone and that others had navigated similar challenges and emerged stronger. In addition to seeking support, I submerged myself in volunteer work, which not only kept me busy, but also gave me a renewed sense of purpose. Engaging in volunteer activities allowed me to give back to the community and stay connected with others.

During this time, I also pursued secondary education, applying for and being accepted into a master's degree program that aligns with my passions and values. This new educational journey has been instrumental in redefining my career path and rekindling my enthusiasm for future possibilities. In comparison to other life stressors, the loss of a job can be particularly destabilizing because it often impacts multiple aspects of one's life, including financial security, social connections, and personal identity.

However, just as one would seek treatment and support for physical health issues or relationship problems, seeking help and building a support network is vital for overcoming the emotional and psychological impact of job loss. Being laid off after fifteen years was undeniably one of the most challenging experiences of my life. Yet it also became an opportunity for introspection and growth. By reflecting on the experience, adopting empowering language, leaning on my support network, and immersing myself in volunteer work and further education, I began to see the potential for new beginnings.

While the stress of losing a job is immense and multifaceted, it is possible to navigate it with resilience and emerge on the other side with renewed strength and purpose. Importantly, I understood what my friend Molly meant when she said, "*My value is not tied to productivity.*" I have value simply because I exist.

Resilience Amidst Political Division

I have more than a few bumper stickers on my car. Most of them are related to human rights, but some lean toward the nerdier side of my personality. My current favorites include a small sticker with a drawing of an opossum and the words: "My stomach hurts and I'm mad at the government," and a larger sticker featuring a raccoon with the phrase: "Caution: Polite but Feral." These stickers serve as both a personal outlet and a subtle form of protest against the tumultuous political climate that has increasingly dominated our national discourse.

The current state of affairs in America feels like a never-ending cycle of frustration and division. The rise of extreme partisanship, the intensification of hate toward those who are different, the onslaught of anti-LGBTQIA+ legislation, and the relentless attacks on reproductive rights and access have left many of us disheartened. The constant barrage of negative rhetoric, coupled with the daily reminders of how fragmented our society has become, can be overwhelming. Yet amid this discomfort, there is an enduring lesson about perseverance and resilience. The long-term benefit of pushing through this challenging period is not merely about enduring discomfort for its own sake, but rather about fostering a deeper sense of empathy and understanding that can lead to meaningful change.

Firstly, facing the current political climate head-on can help cultivate resilience. It is easy to feel disheartened and want to retreat when confronted with hostility and division. However, we contribute to a culture of understanding by continuing to engage in constructive dialogue, such as open debates, respectful disagreements, and active listening, and standing up for principles of inclusivity and respect. This perseverance is not without its trials; it requires us to remain steadfast in our values despite adversity. Over time, this resilience builds a stronger, more compassionate community.

Secondly, pushing through today's discomfort allows us to advocate more effectively for change. When we stand up against injustice and work through the difficulties of a polarized environment, we sharpen our capacity to empathize with others. This empathy, a powerful force, becomes a tool for fostering connections across divides and addressing the root causes of hatred and division. It enables us to approach conflicts with a greater understanding of different perspectives, contributing to more effective and lasting solutions.

Lastly, enduring through tough times can inspire future generations to continue the fight for equity and justice. When we push through current challenges, we set an example of perseverance and commitment. This example can motivate others to join the cause, creating a ripple effect that strengthens collective efforts toward positive change. By demonstrating that it is possible to persist through discomfort and make a difference, we lay the groundwork for a more equitable and compassionate society.

Writing strongly worded letters to legislators, community leaders, and business owners can only get us so far. While these letters are important for expressing our concerns and advocating for change, they are just one piece of a much larger puzzle. The real impact often comes from the persistent, everyday actions we take to promote understanding and bridge divides. Engaging in face-to-face conversations, participating in community initiatives, and supporting grassroots movements play a crucial role in driving meaningful progress.

While the current political climate may feel disheartening and overwhelming, pushing through this discomfort is crucial for fostering resilience, empathy, and long-term change. By remaining committed to our values and continuing to advocate for inclusivity and justice, we contribute to a more positive and unified future. The journey may be arduous, but the long-term benefits of perseverance can transform challenges into opportunities for growth and progress.

From the Podium

Whenever I attend a live testimonial hearing during a legislative session, I am struck by the profound ways our state's legislation shapes the lives of Kansans. These sessions are more than just formalities; they are arenas where real stories are told, and real lives are impacted. The room is often filled with a mix of tension and hope as advocates, legislators, and citizens come together to discuss issues that matter deeply to them. The air is thick with anticipation as people from all levels of society gather to share their experiences, hoping to influence the decisions that will affect their futures.

Each testimony is a powerful reminder of the human element behind every policy decision. The stories shared from the podium are not just anecdotes; they are lived realities, often filled with both struggle and triumph, which highlight the immediate and far-reaching consequences of legislative actions. It is here, in these moments, that I truly understand the power of advocacy and the critical importance of our collective voices. For instance, during one hearing, I listened to a parent of a transgender child from a city located hours away from mine speak out against proposed legislation that threatened her child's safety in school and their ability to live authentically.

In the brief two to three minutes she had, her love and devotion shone through, overpowering the grief and anger such harmful bills evoke. Her voice, though strained with emotion, carried the weight of her family's journey—the fears they faced, the battles they fought, and the unwavering support she offered her child. Her testimony was a poignant reminder of the stakes involved and the human cost of discriminatory policies. I, too, have stood at the podium addressing senators and pleading with state representatives. In those moments, I shared as much of myself as I could, striving to convey why targeting and hurting an already vulnerable community is not only distasteful, but potentially life-threatening.

I recounted personal stories, highlighted statistics, and presented arguments designed to appeal to both the hearts and minds of those in power. The act of speaking out, baring my soul in a room full of decision-makers, is both daunting and empowering. It is a call to action, a plea for empathy, and a demand for justice all rolled into one. The hardest part is listening to those who support hateful legislation, especially when backed by prejudiced legislators. Hearing willful ignorance and prejudice directed at a community I deeply care about is profoundly painful. It is difficult to endure the casual dismissal of our humanity, the unfounded fears and misconceptions, and the blatant disregard for the well-being of others. It is these moments of opposition that strengthen the resolve to continue fighting for what is right.

Despite these challenges, I find hope and strength in these experiences. Witnessing the courage of parents and allies standing up for their loved ones fills me with a sense of purpose. It reminds me that our efforts are not in vain and that our voices, united in love and justice, can bring about positive change. The bravery of those testifying, despite personal risks, showcases strong community bonds. It is a powerful affirmation that even in the face of seemingly insurmountable obstacles, there is always a reason to hope and a reason to fight.

Intentional gladness comes from recognizing these moments of bravery and solidarity. It is about choosing to focus on the love and resilience that drive us to advocate for a better world. In the face of adversity, we find joy in our collective determination to protect and uplift one another. This joy is not naïve optimism, but a steadfast belief in the power of human connection and the possibility of a more just and equitable society. It is a celebration of the progress we have made, and a commitment to the work that still lies ahead.

By continuing to show up, to speak out, and to support one another, we honor the spirit of those who have come before us and pave the way for future generations. From the podium to the streets, our voices rise together in a chorus of hope and determination, echoing the enduring truth that love will always be stronger than hate.

Disclaimer: This next story includes an incident involving sexual assault. I do not recall if I have ever shared my experience fully before, but I will not get into specific details of the incident here. This story focuses primarily on the theme of cultivating resilience. Please feel empowered to skip ahead to the activity if this topic is too much for you.

<3

Let It Hurt, Let It Heal, Let It Go

My first official job as a young person was working at the front desk at a health club. It was a fun job for a high school kid; I made minimum wage—$4.25 per hour. I lived at home with my parents, and the small paychecks were mostly for spending cash and learning about the responsibilities that come with having a checking account. I worked every Wednesday night from 5 p.m. to 10 p.m. and every Saturday from about 7 a.m. until closing (6 or 7 p.m.). I never got a lunch break on my Saturday shift, but I did not know I was supposed to. There were a couple of sweet older members of the gym who would bring me snacks, and on many occasions, I would order pizza to be delivered to me at work—which I would devour in front of all the people trying their hardest to get in shape.

During my shifts, I would clean exercise equipment, change out towels in the locker rooms and pool area, sell health food snacks to members, and, if it was slow, I would read or do my homework. When it was time to toss out the old magazines, I would use the pages I liked best to make collages. I was the only employee at the club during most of my shifts, minus exercise class instructors occasionally showing up to collect their paychecks. Sometimes my boss would pop in for something in his office, but he did not stick around for long, so I had no supervision at work. Just like with lunch breaks, I did not know if I was supposed to have a boss around. Based on my previous work experience as a babysitter, I was used to being the only employee.

I got excited whenever parents came in to work out and brought their teenage kids; unless they were swimming, they would usually hang out up front with me, a fellow teenager. One evening, a guy who usually came in with his parents and younger sister brought a relative with him. He told me that his relative liked me and thought I was cute. I was flattered; this was not something I was used to hearing.

Ten minutes before the gym closed, I did my regular walk through the building to let our members know it was time to get ready to go. I first walked through the weight room, the pool area, and the locker rooms. I would do this walk-through once more at closing to make sure anyone who had not been paying attention, had headphones on, or was in the restroom during my first walk-through knew it was time to go. This evening, the relative of my acquaintance asked if he could go with me during my final walk-through.

This was the first time I ever had anyone with me during a closing walk-through. I had never thought to ask anyone to join me before, but I trusted this guy because I thought I knew his family. I locked the door at closing; anyone who was left in the building during my final walk-through would have to wait at the entrance for me to make my way back to the front so I could unlock the door and let them out. Usually there were only one or two stragglers, the same older folks who brought me snacks. Oddly enough, neither of them came in to work out that night.

I remember walking through the weight room first because it was located behind the check-in desk. I picked up and put away the equipment that got left out. I walked through the empty pool room and checked the sauna and the locker rooms. The building appeared to be empty except for me and my new friend. Years of repression have clouded the remainder of my memories from that night.

I spent so much of my life acting as if this experience was not my own that I cannot remember where we were standing when he grabbed me. I do remember noticing that he and I were the same height when he forced his lips against mine. I tried to push him away, but he barely budged. We might have been the same height, but he was much stronger than me. He shoved me to the floor. I remember the floor was carpeted, but that did not make my landing soft. I recall struggling but I do not remember shouting for help.

Maybe I was too afraid, or maybe I realized it would not matter since we were alone in the building. I do not know if I berated myself at that moment for thinking it was safe to agree to be alone in the building with someone who was a stranger, but I sure did plenty of that in the years that followed.

I only started to allow myself to think about the events of that night when the #MeToo movement began to build momentum and I realized others had experienced a trauma similar to mine. I was glad to know that I was not alone. I hate that anyone experiences sexual assault, but I recognize that with any trauma, it is so much better to heal alongside others with shared experiences.

Letting go of this hurt took a lot of intentional effort. I had to be vulnerable and sit with my trauma and allow myself to feel whatever I needed to feel. This is my story and my journey to acceptance. Each person must walk their own path and heal in their own way. It can be hard to believe that our feelings are valid in a situation where so often the victim is blamed.

Before working through this, I may not have felt that I would find anything to be glad about, but I have identified two things. First, while I have had to work through struggles with intimacy, I am glad this experience did not break my spirit. Second, I am glad that I am here to tell my story; many victims of sexual assault are not that lucky.

am i not a free person?

am I not a free person? do i

not deserve bodily autonomy? why

are others making laws

changing laws that revoke

my rights? how does this

mirror my mother's

mother's experiences?

is my acceptance

as a person on condition

that I make use

of my uterus? is now not

the time for rebellion?

Te toca a ti! – It's your turn!

When you experience trauma, reach out to a trusted friend or professional for support. Reflect on those experiences. Are you committed to healing and resilience? If so, consider language like, "I'm healing" instead of, "I'm broken." This subtle shift reinforces the idea that you are not a prisoner to your trauma. Sharing your experiences and feelings in a safe environment can help you process and heal from trauma.

Reflect on a recent obstacle or roadblock you have encountered. Write down any progress or improvements you made while dealing with it and reframe the setback as an opportunity for growth. This helps shift your focus from perfection to resilience and personal development. Be kind to yourself when things do not go perfectly. Everyone faces setbacks, and these setbacks do not define your worth or potential for growth.

Chapter 10

A Pollyanna State of Mind

*Discover the joy of being fully immersed in
purpose and gladness activities.*

Picture a world where individuals do not just pursue their goals with determination, but with a profound sense of joy and purpose. Imagine a life where actions are driven not by mere obligation, but by compassion, vision, and a genuine sense of gladness.

Purpose and gladness are not distant or conflicting ideals. They are companions on the journey of a meaningful and fulfilling life. When we align our actions with our deepest values and passions, we not only achieve our goals, but also experience true joy and satisfaction.

In the pages that follow, we will explore how living with purpose and gladness can inspire, motivate, and create a positive ripple effect, enriching our own lives and the lives of those around us.

Hotel California

As a human rights activist, I have had multiple opportunities to provide both in-person and written testimony against anti-LGBTQIA+ legislation. For example, one of these bills aimed to prevent genderqueer and transgender children from participating on sports teams that match their gender identities. When hateful legislation like this pops up, I become compelled to show up at the capitol building and provide support for my LGBTQIA+ community. Activism is grueling work. It often feels as though every time you take a step forward, someone immediately shoves you two steps back. Each step forward, however small, makes the fight worth it. I feel glad even in the most minor of victories.

Just days after losing my job, a fellow activist asked me to show up at the statehouse and provide in-person testimony against this hateful legislation. My decision was immediate—not only would I drive to the capitol to speak, but I'd also stay for the hearing of another anti-LGBTQIA+ bill the following day. I confirmed with my spouse that my decision would not cause any schedule conflicts and then went online to pick a hotel within walking distance of the capitol building. I picked the first hotel on the list; it was affordable and only a couple of blocks away. How perfect!

Oh gosh, was I in for a surprise. When I arrived, I observed that the hotel was beyond geriatric. I parked and walked to the front of the building. When I got to the entrance, I noticed a sign taped to the front door indicating that keycard use was required to access the building; but the door was ajar, so I walked inside. Two individuals were at the front desk engrossed in a discussion. As I stood at the counter waiting for service, the two employees disregarded me and continued to debate the pros and cons of split-level heating/AC units. I thought the conversation was interesting as my family has incorporated split-level units in three rooms of our house, so I was patient and waited for the chance to politely interject at the appropriate time.

Unfortunately, I was immediately alerted to the fact that my bladder had other ideas. I began to sway uncomfortably in the lobby, bags hanging over my shoulder, suitcase forgotten at my side, hoping that one of the employees would take notice of my odd behavior and help. As the minutes ticked away, my mind wandered and I began to suspect that this hotel was haunted. The front desk folks were surely poltergeists playing a trick on me. I left my luggage sitting in the lobby and began to wander around in search of a public restroom. I quickly located one off to the side of the reception area. *What luck!* I reached out to open the door—locked. I regretted my decision to avoid stops during the drive to save time. I ran around the corner and—poltergeists be darned—I interjected. "I'm a guest but before I check in, may I please have the key to your restroom?!"

After checking in, I was notified that my room was not yet ready. This made complete sense since I had arrived at 10:30 in the morning. I asked to leave my bags locked at the front desk and took off for the statehouse. When I arrived back at the hotel several hours later, the front door was still ajar. I retrieved my room key from the front desk clerk; this time my presence was acknowledged as soon as I got to the desk. I typically take the stairs when I am staying on the first three floors of a hotel, but when I made it to the staircase with my luggage in tow, it was pitch black. I considered an attempt to locate a light switch, but opted to backtrack and take the elevator.

The elevator groaned and creaked the entire trip up to the second floor. One might assume the ride to be quick; alas, it was an eternity. Once I safely escaped the elevator, I decided that I would search for the light switch before risking another ride in that danger box. As I walked along the corridor, I got the sense that this hotel used to be a boarding house or a long-term community space. There were not many rooms on the floor, and I supposed that each of the rooms were all large.

My hotel room was divided into five spaces: a kitchen area, living room, walk-out balcony, bathroom, and bedroom. I think it may have been larger than the first house my spouse and I lived in early in our marriage. When I stay at a hotel, I like to take a tour of my room and get a feel for the space. There was a sofa chair with a footstool and a larger three-person sofa in the living room. I walked over to the larger sofa and my eyes widened in surprise. The sofa appeared to have collapsed in itself, cushions askew, and the bottom of the sofa was missing!

I shook my head in disbelief and continued my self-guided tour. The kitchen space appeared to be fine, but the balcony was covered in cobwebs that may have been there for several generations of spider births. There was no way I was stepping out there, which truly was a bummer since I had imagined myself sitting outside the following morning sipping a coffee and planning my talking points for the hearing. But it would be okay because rain was in the forecast, so I could be glad there was a table in the kitchen for me to sit at and enjoy my coffee.

The bathroom space was clean, and the bedroom appeared to be okay. Then I noticed some crumbs on the floor in front of the television. I opted to investigate a little further and discovered more crumbs under the table beside the bed. Since I did not see any bugs or rodents, I decided not to bring it to the attention of the front desk person; I could make the best of it. At least I was sleeping inside and not outside in the rain. By 7:30 p.m., I was so exhausted that I decided to climb into bed. I found more crumbs in the bed when I pulled the comforter and sheets back. This would probably be the time that the average person who chose to ignore all the other red flags might choose to request another room.

If I had not been so dang tired, I might have done just that; instead, I brushed the crumbs out of the bed and climbed in fully clothed. As my head made its way toward the pillow, I pulled my hoodie up to protect my short locks from any potentially nefarious thing that might be hiding in the bed with me. It was not a restful sleep. I got up in the morning, bleary-eyed, and made breakfast. I packed up all my stuff, planning to check out from the hotel before heading back to the capitol building. The rain that was promised the evening before came down in sheets.

I remembered a door on the side of the hotel that was considerably closer to my parked car than the front entrance, so I grabbed my belongings and exited the hotel room. I headed for the darkened staircase and carefully made my way down, deliberately dragging my luggage behind me. *Step. Thud. Step. Thud. Step. Thud.* It was a lot of steps. After safely making my way downstairs, I wandered the darkened hallway. I had used an abandoned staircase and was then passing through an unused portion of the hotel. At last, I found the door I had noticed on my walk inside the day before! I walked up to the door, placed my hand on the knob and turned.

The knob turned slightly but then it caught. The door was locked. I looked up and noticed that there was a piece of paper taped to the outside of this door, again stating a keycard was required. I shifted my belongings from my left arm unsteadily to my right arm so I could fish the keycard nestled in my back left pants pocket. I put the keycard up to the black keycard reader. The light turned green but nothing happened. I tried again and then noticed that the door was locked with a deadbolt that required a regular key to unlock. It was then that I momentarily gave into the feeling of uncertainty; my heart began to race. Was I trapped in this hotel? What if there had been a fire? I had not even found my way back to the front door.

At this last thought, I laughed out loud at the complete weirdness of this hotel stay and began to trace my way back to the stairs. Up the stairs I went. *Step. Thud. Step. Thud. Step. Thud.* After several more minutes of searching, I found a lit staircase, made my way downstairs, and located the exit. I smiled—perhaps a little too widely—at the employee tending the counter, gently tossed my keycard down, and called over my shoulder as I walked out the door that I was checking out. What does this long-winded story have to do with the Glad Game, you ask? Well, I was sure glad that I made it out alive and incident-free. Plus, it is a fun story to tell, since I did not die. It sure was an adventure.

Rediscovering the Power of Journaling

Journaling is a mighty helpful tool for self-reflection and growth. Yet amidst the demands of daily life, I found myself drifting away from it. Recently, I decided to reintegrate journaling into my routine with a novel approach: writing just one sentence a day, focusing on gratitude and positivity. This simple yet profound shift aimed to foster a more optimistic outlook and enhance my overall well-being. My commitment to this concise approach made the practice manageable and sustainable, even on the busiest days. The focus on gratitude and positivity guided each entry, allowing me to concentrate on the bright spots of my daily life rather than any overwhelming negatives. This shift in perspective was both refreshing and enlightening.

Inevitably, there are days when it feels impossible to find something positive to write about. On these days, I allow myself to acknowledge the difficulty and be honest about my feelings.

Instead of forcing a positive spin, I write a sentence reflecting my current state, even if it is simply acknowledging that today was tough. This approach honors my feelings without undermining the practice of finding something to appreciate. Over time, this honesty contributes to personal growth and resilience.

On better days, I focus on reflecting on something positive or an aspect of my life for which I feel grateful. Writing down these reflections, even in their simplest form, became a ritual that encouraged mindfulness and appreciation. This daily practice helped me recognize and celebrate the small joys and successes that might otherwise go unnoticed. By concentrating on positive aspects, I nurtured a more optimistic mindset and cultivated resilience in the face of challenges.

The impact of this minimalist journaling practice was profound. Focusing on gratitude and positivity not only brightened my daily outlook, but also reinforced a sense of contentment and well-being. Writing a single sentence allowed me to appreciate the positive elements of my life more fully and acknowledge the progress I was making, no matter how small. This practice provided a gentle reminder that even on challenging days, there is always something worth appreciating or, at the very least, a lesson to be learned.

Recommitting to journaling with a focus on gratitude and positivity has been a transformative experience. This approach has highlighted the power of small, consistent actions in fostering a more optimistic outlook and deeper self-awareness. As I continue this practice, I remain committed to celebrating the positive aspects of life and embracing the journey with gratitude, even on the tough days. The simplicity of writing one sentence a day made the practice accessible and meaningful, fostering a greater sense of appreciation and resilience. I have learned to navigate life's ups and downs with a more positive mindset by concentrating on what I am grateful for and acknowledging difficult days.

Gratitude: There's an App for That

My son introduced me to an app that I am in love with called Finch. Finch is a self-care and mental wellness app designed to support individuals in building healthy habits, managing stress, and improving their overall well-being. It features a virtual pet—a cute bird named Finch (you can choose your bird's name) that users take care of by completing various self-care activities. The app offers daily check-ins, mood tracking, journaling prompts, breathing exercises, and goal-setting tools to encourage people to engage in positive behaviors. As individuals complete these activities, they earn rewards that help their Finch grow and thrive. The gamified approach makes self-care more engaging and motivating for people like me who need a reminder.

Using Finch brings back fond memories of my high school days when I had a Tamagotchi. Just like my Tamagotchi, Finch requires regular attention and care, creating a similar sense of responsibility and attachment. However, Finch goes beyond being simply a digital pet by incorporating self-care activities that improve my mental well-being. My favorite part of the Finch app is that it provides me with simple ways to connect with friends and family members who also use the app. Each morning, I can send my little brother a "thinking of you" message, my son a "good morning," and my friends a reminder to "drink water" or even a "grateful for you." When I send messages to others, it reminds me to do those things for myself.

By expressing appreciation and sending these thoughtful messages, I have noticed a deeper sense of connection with my loved ones. These small acts of kindness not only brighten our day, but also remind us of the importance of nurturing relationships. It is incredible how a simple "thinking of you" or "grateful for you" message can strengthen bonds and create a sense of mutual support. Reflecting on my experiences with Finch, I realized how much gratitude has become an integral part of my daily routine. Before using the app, I often found myself caught up in the hustle and bustle of everyday life, neglecting to pause and appreciate the small joys and blessings around me. Finch has encouraged me to take a moment each day to reflect on what I am grateful for, and this practice has profoundly impacted my mindset.

Gratitude has helped me manage stress more effectively. Focusing on the things I am thankful for offers a sense of perspective. It reminds me that there is always something positive to hold onto during challenging times. Whether it is appreciating a beautiful sunrise, the support of my family, or the opportunity to engage in self-care activities through Finch, these moments of gratitude serve as a source of comfort. The journaling prompts in the app have been particularly helpful in fostering my gratitude practice. I have developed a habit of focusing on each positive aspect of my life by taking a few minutes each day to write down what I am grateful for. This simple practice has propelled me forward and made me even more aware of the abundance of blessings surrounding me.

Practicing gratitude through the Finch app has transformed my daily routine and overall outlook on life. It has encouraged me to pause more frequently to appreciate the small joys, strengthened relationships, and provided me with a powerful tool for managing stress. Expressing gratitude truly is a key component of cultivating a positive, purposeful mindset, and I am grateful for the opportunity to embrace this practice through the Finch app.

Living a Life of Intentional Gladness

Passion, authenticity, and determination are pivotal to my pursuit of intentional gladness. These qualities propel me toward a life well-lived, infused with enthusiasm, genuine connections, and resilience in overcoming challenges. They form the bedrock of my journey toward purposeful living and finding joy in every endeavor. I see passion as the intense enthusiasm and dedication we bring to our pursuits. It is the fuel that drives us to achieve our goals and pursue our dreams. Passion gives me a sense of purpose and motivation, making my endeavors meaningful and fulfilling.

To cultivate passion, we can start by identifying what truly excites and inspires us. Engaging in activities that align with our interests and values can help us stay connected to our passion. By applying passion in our daily lives, we can infuse our actions with energy and enthusiasm, spreading gladness to those around us. Throughout my life,

I have embraced my passion—being high-energy, high-enthusiasm, and having little patience for closed-mindedness. Whether it is initiating new projects or engaging in discussions, I approach them all with an unmatched vigor. My friend Rosa often remarks that my high energy can be overwhelming for some people, as not everyone is prepared for the intensity that I bring into any room I enter, either physically or virtually.

I dive into projects with a fervor that inspires action and momentum. When I am passionate about a cause or idea, I channel my energy into driving it forward, often motivating others to join in. This level of enthusiasm is not just a personality trait but a driving force behind my pursuit of meaningful goals and initiatives. Another character trait that I view as essential to living a life of intentional gladness is authenticity: the quality of being genuine and true to oneself. It involves embracing our true selves, including our strengths and vulnerabilities, without fear of judgment. Authenticity fosters trust and deep connections with others, as it encourages openness and honesty.

To cultivate authenticity, we can practice self-awareness, reflect on our values, and express our true thoughts and feelings. By living authentically, we create an environment where others feel comfortable being themselves, inspiring a sense of acceptance and gladness. For me, being authentic means expressing my thoughts and feelings honestly, even when they challenge others' perspectives or expectations. For instance, in discussions or decision-making processes, I prioritize transparency and clarity, ensuring that my actions align with my values and beliefs. This approach fosters trust and genuine connections with those who appreciate honesty and sincerity.

I have also recognized the importance of balancing authenticity with empathy and tact. My authenticity can sometimes intimidate people because I speak my mind and stand by my words. While this trait is not inherently negative, it requires careful navigation to avoid creating unintended rifts in relationships that are still developing. By understanding different viewpoints and communicating respectfully, I strive to build bridges rather than unintentionally causing friction. My commitment to authenticity serves as a cornerstone in nurturing meaningful relationships grounded in mutual respect and understanding.

A third key characteristic to a life lived in a Pollyanna state of mind is determination:

that unwavering resolve to achieve our goals despite obstacles and setbacks. It is the quality that keeps me moving forward, even when the journey is challenging. This determination helps me stay focused and committed, allowing me to overcome difficulties and achieve success. To build determination, we can set clear goals, break them down into manageable steps, and maintain a positive mindset. By embodying determination, we inspire others to pursue their aspirations with tenacity, resilience, and gladness.

My determination often pairs closely with my curiosity, driving me to explore new opportunities and push boundaries. When I set my sights on a goal, I approach it with unwavering resolve and a relentless desire to learn and grow. Years ago, when I became drawn to human rights advocacy, particularly for LGBTQIA+ youth, I first immersed myself in research. I sought out mentors and attended workshops to deepen my understanding. My curiosity fueled my determination to persevere. I pursued certifications, collaborated with experts in the LGBTQIA+ community, and eventually joined the board of an advocacy organization. This opportunity allowed me to effect meaningful change in my community and empowered me to advocate passionately for the rights and well-being of LGBTQIA+ youth.

This blend of determination and curiosity not only propels me towards achieving my goals, but also fuels my passion for continuous improvement and innovation. It allows me to embrace challenges as opportunities for personal and professional growth, inspiring others to join me on the journey toward meaningful change. To integrate these qualities into my life and cultivate intentional gladness, I start by setting daily intentions. Each morning, I reflect on how I want to embody passion, authenticity, and determination throughout the day. I also seek out interactions or practice these qualities—whether it is by pursuing my interests with enthusiasm, being true to myself in every interaction, or persevering through challenges with resolve.

By regularly checking in with ourselves, we can ensure that we are living in alignment with our purpose and fostering a sense of gladness in our lives and the lives of those around us. Embracing our gladness qualities can transform our mindset and help us navigate life's journey with joy and meaning. Cultivating passion, authenticity, and determination is essential to leading a purposeful and glad life.

what is an hour?

i never knew the value of time

until i had one hour each week to fill

that time became very special to me - it was

a time to plan and to prepare for what's to come

a time to mindlessly scroll on social media

a time to listen to music or audiobook

a time to attend a virtual meeting

a time to catch up on email

a time to think to reflect

a time to sit in silence

a time to meditate

a time to read

a time to cry

a time to be

Te toca a ti! – It's your turn!

Practice gratitude. Gratitude is a key component of the Glad Game and can also be helpful for cultivating a positive, purposeful mindset. Take some time each day to reflect on things you are grateful for as a human. This can be done through journaling, meditation, or simply taking a few moments to pause and appreciate the good things in your life. Express gratitude to others in your life, whether through a thank-you note, a compliment, or a simple expression of appreciation.

Reflect on your journey so far. How will you embrace future challenges and opportunities with optimism and intentional gladness to "Be More Pollyanna" in your daily life?

Afterword

As I put the final touches on *Be More Pollyanna*, I found myself reflecting on the incredible journey that brought this book to life. Writing about intentional gladness has been as much a personal exploration as a message to share. It has reminded me that optimism is not a passive state but a deliberate choice we can make daily despite life's challenges. Thank you for embarking on this journey with me. Whether you've read this book in a single sitting or returned to its pages over time, I hope it has sparked something within you—a sense of possibility, a desire to seek joy, or simply a moment of quiet reflection. I wish that you carry the spirit of Pollyanna in your own unique way, spreading gladness and resilience wherever you go.

At the end of July 2024, nearly 18 months after my unexpected catalyst for change occurred, I found myself in a tattoo shop, mere days before embarking on a new career, to discuss my addition of a tattoo of the most important message I have ever learned: *DON'T PANIC*. I first read this statement in my youth as a seventh grader. I clearly remember wandering through the aisles of my middle school library, doing what I do to this day—waiting for the right book to call out to me. My life was forever changed when I discovered *The Hitchhiker's Guide to the Galaxy,* written by the late Douglas Adams. I left the shop that evening with a permanent reminder on my right forearm.

The first two years of my forties have been unexpected, enlightening, and unbelievable. I wake up every day and head to a job I am deeply passionate about, where I have the privilege of working alongside dedicated individuals to create a positive impact in our community. This role challenges and inspires me and allows me to align my professional efforts with my values. At the same time, I am a master's student pursuing a graduate degree program that has brought me immense joy. The coursework, the camaraderie of my peers, and the opportunity to dive deeper into subjects I care about have been transformative. These experiences have reinforced my belief in lifelong learning and the power of pursuing one's passions.

As I reflect on the themes of optimism and resilience that run through this book, I find myself, even now, reinvigorated to fight injustice. The constant barrage of anti-LGBTQIA+ and other dehumanizing legislation presented locally and within the walls of Capitol Hill is a stark reminder of the ongoing challenges faced by marginalized communities. This fight is personal; it is a call to action—a reminder that the work of advocating for equity and kindness is never finished. Through intentional gladness, I find the strength to persist, resist, and imagine a brighter future for everyone.

If this book has resonated with you, I invite you to stay connected. You can find me at hollyterrill.com, where I share updates, musings, and opportunities to engage in community advocacy. I would love to hear how *Be More Pollyanna* has impacted your life and the ways you are cultivating gladness in your corner of the world. Finally, I leave you with a thought that guided me throughout this process: *Optimism is not about ignoring life's difficulties but finding the light within them. It's about choosing to believe in better days, in ourselves, and in each other*. Thank you for letting this book be part of your story. Now, go forth and shine with gratitude and gladness.

Holly Terrill,
January 2025

About the Author

Holly Terrill (She/They) is a writer, leader, and advocate dedicated to personal and community growth. With nearly two decades of nonprofit experience, Holly strives to improve lives and spark positive change. Their openness about their personal journey fosters deep connections with others.

As Executive Director of Bike Walk Wichita, Holly works to ensure safe, accessible transportation for everyone, especially those often overlooked. Believing in the transformative power of active transportation, Holly's work is rooted in creating stronger, more connected neighborhoods.

Holly is a passionate advocate for safer, more inclusive spaces through activism with GLSEN, promoting equity for LGBTQIA+ students in schools. Outside work, Holly enjoys spending time with their family. Holly lives in Wichita, Kansas, with their spouse, son, and three dogs. Through their work, writing, and everyday interactions, they hope to inspire others to #BeMorePollyanna.

Acknowledgments

Oh heck, I am going to forget to thank someone who helped me on this path, but here it goes! Out of the multitudes of literature available, thank YOU for choosing this book. A bear hug-sized thank you to Ben—my spouse, partner, and best friend—and to my incredible, tenacious son Maison. I love you both! You are my motivation, and inspire me to be my best self every day.

This book would not exist without the love and support of so many people. To my family, friends, and mentors, thank you for encouraging me to embrace my authentic self and pursue my dreams. To the incredible team at Quiet Storm Services, your belief in this manuscript means the world to me. And to my community at Bike Walk Wichita and GLSEN, thank you for teaching me the power of collective action and hope.

Thanks to my folks for encouraging me to keep going when I first brought them my early writing, and for proudly posting my poems on the refrigerator (there's still one on there today!) Thank you to my brother, Davis Jr.—writer, actor, director, stunt coordinator, and an all-around great dude, who sets an excellent example for how to follow one's passions.

Heartfelt gratitude to my BFF and forever work-wife, Rosa. You always push me to succeed while calling me out on my crap. I am a published author because you encouraged me to share my leadership experience with the world in 2020. I love you! Thank you to my circle of awe-inspiring friends for consistently supporting my many aspirational (and often nerdy) whims. Thanks to all my workplace proximity associates (current and former); you create collaborative and fun workplaces, where all belong.

Much appreciation to author Julie Kenner, who encouraged me to "Keep writing, no matter what," when I reached out for advice on MySpace during the early days of social media. Thank you to Trader Joe's for your tasty gluten-free bagels, hot chocolate cream cheese, and everything bagel seasoning—the official snack food of my writing journey. Please bring back the hot chocolate cream cheese!

Thanks to my disembodied robot pal Kevin, better known as ChatGPT, an AI language model developed by OpenAI, for assisting me with organizing my themes and activities. Your guidance was surprisingly helpful! Lastly, a hearty thanks to every person who has called me "Pollyanna." I hope you find this book and that it helps you identify something for which to be glad about each day.

References

Baty, Chris. (2006). The No Plot? No Problem! Novel-Writing Kit. Chronicle Books.

Declaration of Independence: A Transcription. The U.S. National Archives and Records

Administration. https://www.archives.gov/founding-docs/declaration-transcript

[The] Declaration of Independence: What Does it Say? The U.S. National Archives and Records Administration.

https://www.archives.gov/founding-docs/declaration/what-does-it-say

Porter, E. H. (2003). Pollyanna. Dover.

Rubin, Gretchen. (2009). The Happiness Project. HarperCollins.

SARK (2010). Glad No Matter What. New World Library.

Terrill, H. January 04, 2023. Contact Center Leader's Advice to Their Younger Self. ICMI. Contact Center Insider.

https://www.icmi.com/resources/2023/advice-to-young-contact-center-leaders

Terrill, H. April 06, 2021. Pandemic Lessons in Parenthood and Leadership. ICMI. Contact Center Insider.

https://www.icmi.com/resources/2021/pandemic-lessons-parenthood-leadership

Terrill, H. November 11, 2020. Contact Center Leaders: Secure Your Mask First. ICMI. Contact Center Insider.

https://www.icmi.com/resources/2020/secure-your-own-mask-first

Resources

For a comprehensive list of resources, please visit:

www.bemorepollyanna.com

www.quietstormservices.com/resources